The Case for Monarchy

By Gen Ponce

First edition.

Introduction: The Forgotten Wisdom of Christendom

It is undeniable that the Western governments of the twentieth and twenty first centuries have failed. Failed to secure the common good, failed to protect their peoples, and failed to maintain peace. The consistent disregard for the well being of the common people has made it obvious that these Western governments are not merely incompetent, but malicious. Of course, the situation could be worse. At least we no longer live under the tyrannical rule of a theocratic king, right? How silly it was for peoples of the past to determine who ought to rule merely based on birth, a matter of random happenstance. The modern world has advanced well beyond the archaic notion of hereditary rule, which stripped the lower classes of agency, voting rights, or precious religious freedom. For all the flaws of the modern world, at least we all have *true* liberty, right?

It may come as a surprise to the average person that every major institution has lied about this aspect of history. The common narrative goes as follows: for most of recorded history, evil emperors, monarchs, or any flavor of dictator used religion and or other socially imposed standards to cling to power, oppressing women, the poor, minority groups, and all who did not conform to the status quo. This terror of kings, lords, and other powerful classes against less influential groups continued until the so-called Enlightenment, when brilliant thinkers emerged. These intelligent men were revolutionary, suggesting that mankind cannot know that a fact is true unless it is proven beyond all doubt. In other words, these thinkers were the pioneers of the Reddit user's classic response to common sense statements, which typically comes in the form of "Um, do you have a source for that?"

Since the discovery that human reason is not enough to determine truth, it reasonably follows that since there is no way to *prove* the authority of a monarch, he therefore has no real authority at all. The authority of a ruler ought to be *proven* by a majority vote, or from a more right wing perspective, by the vote of the aristocracy. Authority ought only be granted to one who has earned it, being deemed fit to rule not by the

Church, whose authority cannot be *proven* to be true, but by the light of man's reason.

This sounds logical at first. Yet upon deeper examination, this narrative falls flat. In reality, what modernity condemns as cruel, oppressive, and irrational was in fact ordered toward the common good in ways modern democracies have failed to be. Under the Catholic monarchies of the Middle Ages, citizens, including women and minority groups, had rights and protections that democracies ironically fail to provide.

This book is not a glorification of the past. Human nature is corrupt, and so, of course, medieval Christendom was filled with corruption. There were abuses, hardship, and evils of all kinds. Yet this is where the Catholic perspective differs from the modern one. Modern man seeks to create utopia, Heaven on Earth, where man is free to do as he pleases and faces as little suffering as possible. The traditional Catholic, on the other hand, understands that suffering and evil are inevitable, because mankind is not made for this world. Mankind is made for unity with Christ, not for pleasurable earthly existence. Living happily is important, but developing a system of government for the ultimate end of worldly happiness is akin to planning a wedding so that the guests may eat cake. Cake ought to be available at a reception, but it should not be why a couple gets married.

Although I would argue that monarchy, when rightly done, is better for the salvation of souls, this book will not be an argument for the existence of God or a case for the Catholic religion. Instead, I will be arguing that merely living as though Catholicism were true leads to better outcomes in this life than our current system does. Ironically, this is due to the prioritization of the afterlife rather than the prioritization of earthly life. Medieval Christendom understood this, and while they are mocked today by those who likely find the truth of the matter uncomfortable, the reality is that many of their "archaic" systems functioned far better than our "advanced" modern systems of government. The postmodern world can never revive the past, but it would do best to learn from it and, one day, apply these older systems to new societies as best as possible.

Part 1: Misconceptions About Monarchy

Chapter 1: "Monarchy Means Tyranny"

This is the most widespread misconception about monarchy that exists. Many believe that a monarchical system, in which a ruler is assigned authority at birth, will inevitably devolve into tyranny. The logic behind this idea is that a hereditary monarch feels entitled to power and will therefore place his personal interests above those of his citizens. In reality, this tendency appears far more frequently among elected officials, historically speaking.[1]

Elected officials in Western countries are obliged to say whatever is necessary to win the popular vote, then once in office, ignore the will of the people,

---

[1] **Aristotle**, *Politics*, Book V, chapters 10–11
Aristotle explicitly teaches that tyranny most often arises in regimes where rulers seek office through ambition and popular favor, noting that elective systems encourage demagoguery and self interest rather than rule for the common good. See also V-Dem's **Political Corruption Index** provides quantitative, cross-national data on corruption levels that correlate with different political systems, showing democracies with comparatively higher corruption scores in some respects.

since they no longer practically need it to maintain power.[2] When a United States president, whether Republican or Democrat, fails to fulfill his campaign promises, the people merely shrug, falsely assured that whoever they vote into power next will "be better." Yet nothing fundamentally changes.[3] Ironically, it is the elected official who comes to resemble a tyrant, feeling that his arduous efforts to win office earn him the right to impose his own will rather than to serve the will of those he governs.

A king, by contrast, does not earn his power and therefore is far less likely to feel personally entitled

---

[2] **George Washington**, *Farewell Address* (1796) Washington warns that elected officials will manipulate public passions to gain power and then govern according to factional interest rather than the common good. He was arguably proven right by studies such as these: 1) Heck, Luke. "Study: Politicians Vote According to Constituents Only About 35 Percent of the Time." *ProMarket*, 16 June 2017, 2) Pew Research Center. "6. Perceptions of Elected Officials and the Role of Money in Politics." *Pew Research Center: Politics & Policy*, 23 Nov. 2015, 3) Mitchell, Josh. "Americans Don't Think Their Elected Officials Listen to Them." *Stanford News*, 15 Feb. 2018.

[3] **Alexis de Tocqueville**, *Democracy in America*, Vol. I, Part II, ch. 7, Tocqueville observes that democratic peoples repeatedly place hope in new leaders despite structural failures, mistaking rotation of office for real reform. See also, again: Mitchell, Josh. "Americans Don't Think Their Elected Officials Listen to Them." *Stanford News*, 15 Feb. 2018

to it.[4] Corrupt kings have existed, of course, but they are few in number when compared to corrupt presidents, prime ministers, and other elected rulers.[5]

History demonstrates this contrast clearly. Rome, for example, in its late stages, was a republic. Much like in America today, bribery and factionalism were widespread. Figures like Marius, Sulla, and Caesar used elections won by popular support to seize immense power. The Roman Republic collapsed not due to hereditary kingship, but because offices became tools of personal ambition.[6]

The French Revolutionary governments formed similar destructive outcomes. After the abolition of France's monarchy, a series of elected or representative regimes produced mass executions, suppression of religion, military dictatorship, and

---

[4] **St. Thomas Aquinas**, *De Regimine Principum*, Book I, chapter 7, Aquinas argues that hereditary kingship moderates ambition precisely because the ruler does not acquire power through personal striving.

[5] **Sallust**, *The Jugurthine War*, chs. 31–35
Sallust describes widespread bribery, corruption, and moral decay among elected Roman magistrates, contrasting republican ambition with earlier monarchical restraint.

[6] **Ibid,** Book I; **Plutarch**, *Lives* (Marius, Sulla, Caesar). These sources document bribery, electoral corruption, factionalism, and the use of popular support to accumulate extraordinary power in the late Roman Republic.

the infamous Reign of Terror. This all occurred under governments which claimed legitimacy not from God or even royal blood, but from "the people."[7]

Most infamously, the failures of the Weimar Republic in Germany led to the popular rise of Adolf Hitler. The Republic fueled hyperinflation by printing money rather than trying to restore productive order after the Great War. Despite being formally democratic, Weimar Germany was almost ungovernable, plagued by street violence, political assassinations, poverty, prostitution, widespread pornography, and the frequent suspension of civil liberties. The German People are, to this day, demonized for their past support of the Nazi regime. Yet given the state of Germany at the time, who could blame them for such support?[8]

Compare these unstable, anarcho-tyrannical conditions to those of long reigning European monarchs. Saint Louis IX of France, from a young age, was raised to see kingship as a moral burden

---

[7] **Edmund Burke**, *Reflections on the Revolution in France* (1790); **Actes de la Convention nationale* (1792–1794). Burke and the official revolutionary records attest to mass executions, suppression of religion, and the ideological grounding of authority in "the people."

[8] **Oswald Spengler**, *The Decline of the West*, Vol. II (1918–1922); **Gustav Stresemann**, speeches and papers; **Victor Klemperer**, early diaries (1920s).

rather than a prize. He submitted himself to the law, corrected abuses, and ruled with justice. He was a great king precisely because he did not view his crown as a prize he had won, nor as a mark of innate superiority.[9] Saint Edward the Confessor is another great example, ruling as a steward, not a conqueror. His reign was marked by peace and restraint rather than chaos or tyranny. Like Louis IX, he was well aware that his authority was received, not earned.[10] Far more than those two examples, the Capetian kings of France produced remarkable stability for centuries. They were formed from childhood and bound by custom, coronation oaths, and the authority of the Church.[11]

In other words, monarchs were restrained by the Church above and the nobility below. The king

---

[9] **Jean de Joinville**, *Life of Saint Louis*; **St. Thomas Aquinas**, *De Regimine Principum*, Book I. Joinville's eyewitness account and Aquinas's political theology describe Louis IX's understanding of kingship as a moral office ordered to justice and law.

[10] **The Anglo-Saxon Chronicle**; **William of Malmesbury**, *Gesta Regum Anglorum*.
These sources attest to the peaceful character of Edward the Confessor's reign and his conception of kingship as stewardship rather than domination.

[11] **Orderic Vitalis**, *Historia Ecclesiastica*; **Suger of Saint-Denis**, *Life of Louis VI*; *Coronation Ordo of Reims.*
These sources attest to the formation of Capetian kingship, the binding force of coronation oaths, and the integration of royal authority with ecclesiastical sanction.

could never possess absolute power and was corrected when he abused his authority. King John of England is the most famous example of this: a tyrannical ruler restrained by the English barons, the Archbishop of Canterbury, and the Pope. He was famously forced to sign the Magna Carta, seeing his authority corrected rather than abolished.[12]

Kings faced not only the possibility of revolt by the nobility, but the threat of excommunication. Such a penalty carried actual weight when the Church had civil authority. Emperor Henry IV, Philip Augustus of France, and Emperor Frederick II were all excommunicated for serious scandal or for overstepping their bounds. These rulers were curtailed rather than overthrown.[13] One can only imagine how much better modern politicians would behave if excommunication carried any serious temporal consequences.

---

[12] **Magna Carta** (1215); **Roger of Wendover**, *Flores Historiarum*; **Pope Innocent III**, letters to King John. Contemporary records document John's submission to baronial and ecclesiastical correction and the restoration of lawful kingship rather than its abolition.

[13] **Lambert of Hersfeld**, *Annals* (Henry IV); **Pope Innocent III**, letters concerning Philip Augustus; **Matthew Paris**, *Chronica Majora* (Frederick II). These chronicles and papal documents show the real political effects of excommunication and ecclesiastical discipline upon rulers.

Catholic feudal monarchy was not tyranny. It contained checks and balances precisely so that monarchs cannot abuse their power and can only ever use it for the good of the people. At the same time, monarchs were kept in place so that worse figures could not seize power by ambition or through chaos.[14] If this system worked so well, one might then wonder why monarchies were revolted against in the first place.

The apostasy of King Henry VIII marked a turning point in Western history. He broke from the Church, rejected papal authority, confiscated ecclesiastical property, and eliminated independent church courts. The nobility, which had successfully restrained corrupt monarchs in earlier centuries, was already weakened by the Wars of the Roses and by the Tudors' deliberate centralization of power.[15] While noble authority had largely been stripped away before Henry's reign, it was the rejection of the

---

[14] **St. Thomas Aquinas**, *De Regimine Principum*, Book I; **Aristotle**, *Politics*, Book III (as received in medieval political thought). Aquinas explicitly teaches that kingship ordered to the common good is restrained by law and intermediate authorities.

[15] **St. Thomas More**, *History of King Richard III*; **Polydore Vergil**, *Anglica Historia*; **Acts of Henry VII and Henry VIII**, especially statutes on retaining and the Star Chamber. These sources attest to the destruction of the great feudal houses during the Wars of the Roses and the deliberate Tudor policy of neutralizing noble independence.

Church that definitively ushered in state absolutism. When Americans today imagine the tyrannical monarchy that pilgrims and Founding Fathers were fleeing, they are thinking of Henry VIII's invention: not feudal monarchy, but absolute monarchy, stripped of its restraints. By the eve of the French Revolution, France's government had unfortunately devolved in a similar manner.[16]

The problem with the revolutions was not that they rose against tyrannical rulers, but that they dismantled monarchy itself rather than reforming it. Without the nobility, and especially without the Church, the lower classes came to revolt against kings in the same way kings had already revolted against God.[17]

Despite their promises, the revolutions of France and America did not free the lower classes. They worsened their conditions. In France, the abolition

---

[16] **Acts of Supremacy** (1534); **St. Thomas More**, *Letters from the Tower*; **Jean Bodin**, *Six Books of the Commonwealth* (1576). These sources illustrate the English break with ecclesiastical restraint and the theoretical development of absolute sovereignty later mirrored in France.

[17] **Edmund Burke**, *Reflections on the Revolution in France*; **Abbé Sieyès**, *What Is the Third Estate?*. Burke's contemporary analysis contrasts organic monarchy with revolutionary destruction, while Sieyès reveals the ideological logic that severed authority from tradition and the Church.

of feudal protections, guilds, and customary rights was followed by centralized taxation, conscription, and terror. Peasants gained not protections, but slogans. In the end, they were worse off after the Revolution than they were before it.[18]

The American Revolution is extremely overly romanticized. Though its grievances were understandable, it carried many negative consequences as well. Power was consolidated among merchants, bankers, and lawyers when they were no longer restrained by the crown.[19] This resulted in there being no meaningful relief for debtors or small farmers,[20] and eventually the

---

[18] **National Assembly of France**, *Decrees of August 4, 1789*; **Georges Lefebvre**, *The Peasants of the North during the French Revolution* (1924); **Edmund Burke**, *Reflections on the Revolution in France* (1790). These sources document the abolition of feudal rights, the destruction of guilds, increased taxation, conscription, and the worsening condition of peasants after 1789.

[19] **The Federalist Papers**, Nos. 10 and 51 (James Madison); **Gouverneur Morris**, *Diary and Letters*; **Proceedings of the Constitutional Convention of 1787.* These sources reveal the Founders' explicit concern with property holders, commercial interests, and the intentional insulation of governance from popular pressure, resulting in elite consolidation of power.

[20] **Proceedings of the Massachusetts General Court** (1786–1787); **George Washington**, letter to Henry Lee, October 31, 1786; **Thomas Jefferson**, correspondence on Shays' Rebellion. Contemporary documents show the lack of debtor relief, harsh tax enforcement, and the

modern corruption seen in America today.[21] Shays' Rebellion stands as early proof that the lower classes gained no real voice in the new order.[22]

What followed these revolutions was not the liberation of the common man, but his exposure to far more impersonal and unrestrained forms of power. Authority was no longer embodied in a king bound by custom, faith, and law, but dispersed into bureaucracies, assemblies, and financial interests accountable to no one in particular. The promise was liberty; the result was a new tyranny, less visible, more pervasive, and far harder to resist. Democracy did not abolish tyranny, it generalized it. Far from being a tyrant, the king could be resisted. The modern state cannot.[23]

---

violent suppression of agrarian resistance, demonstrating the failure of the new regime to protect small farmers.

[21] **Gen Ponce, *Pigs***. My previous book, titled *Pigs*, traces the long term economic corruption of the modern United States, linking early elite consolidation to present day financial exploitation and systemic injustice.

[22] **Proceedings of the Massachusetts General Court** (1786–1787); **George Washington**, letter to Henry Lee, Oct. 31, 1786; **Thomas Jefferson**, correspondence on Shays' Rebellion. Contemporary records show elite consolidation of power, lack of debtor relief, and the violent suppression of rural unrest.

[23] **Alexis de Tocqueville**, *The Old Regime and the Revolution* (1856); **St. Thomas Aquinas**, *De Regimine Principum*, Book I; **Pope Leo XIII**, *Diuturnum Illud* (1881). Tocqueville explains how revolutionary states centralized power more thoroughly than monarchies,

while Aquinas and Leo XIII provide the theological framework distinguishing lawful authority from modern tyranny.

Chapter 2: "People Had No Rights Under Kings"

A myth that persists to this day is that the lower classes were powerless under kings, especially under feudalism. This myth is further reinforced by the modern assumption that rights only exist where there are elections, in which each individual citizen has a direct say in who holds power.[24]

The modern understanding of "rights" is typically a series of abstract claims granted by the state. Under a liberal framework, these claims amount to the belief that individuals should be legally permitted to do whatever they wish, so long as no "immediate harm" is inflicted on others.[25] The medieval

---

[24] **Alexis de Tocqueville**, *The Old Regime and the Revolution* (1856).
Tocqueville explicitly contrasts modern electoral notions of political participation with the concrete liberties exercised by local bodies and estates under monarchy.
[25] **John Locke**, *Second Treatise of Government*, chs. II–V; **John Stuart Mill**, *On Liberty*. These foundational

understanding of rights was fundamentally different. In the Middle Ages, the rights of man were concrete, inherited, enforceable, and understood as necessary for the flourishing of society.[26] The central irony is that medieval people possessed far fewer slogans than the various liberal movements throughout history, yet enjoyed more real protections and freedoms.[27]

The truth is that rights are not permissions granted by the state, but limits placed upon it.[28] Even America's Founding Fathers understood freedom of speech not as the right to say anything one wishes, but as the right to speak the truth without

---

liberal texts articulate rights primarily as individual permissions defined and protected by civil authority.

[26] **St. Thomas Aquinas**, *Summa Theologiae*, I–II, q. 90–97; **Henry de Bracton**, *De Legibus et Consuetudinibus Angliae*. Aquinas defines law as an ordinance of reason ordered to the common good, while Bracton affirms that the king is under the law and bound by custom and justice.

[27] **Magna Carta** (1215); **Town Charters of medieval France and England**; **Jean de Joinville**, *Life of Saint Louis*. These sources attest to inherited liberties, enforceable legal protections, and the practical security enjoyed by common people under medieval Christian monarchy.

[28] **St. Thomas Aquinas**, *Summa Theologiae*, I–II, q. 90, a. 1; q. 96, a. 4. Aquinas defines law as an ordinance of reason ordered to the common good and teaches that unjust laws exceed authority and lack binding force, thereby limiting the state.

interference from authority.[29] Medieval Europeans likewise understood rights as protections of the common good, not as legal permission to indulge every desire.[30] A mother has the *right* to raise her children without intrusion. A man has the *right* to provide for his family. A priest has the *right* to offer the Liturgy.[31] In short, a right is the freedom to do what is good and reasonable without unjust obstruction. Rights arise from natural law and from God, not from mere human will.

Rights were protected by custom and by the Church, and rather than being the source of the law, the king himself was subject to it.[32] Violating the

---

[29] **James Madison**, *Speech Introducing the Bill of Rights* (June 8, 1789); **John Adams**, *A Dissertation on the Canon and the Feudal Law* (1765). These texts show that early American thinkers understood freedom of speech as protection against governmental suppression of truth, not as license for moral disorder.

[30] **Henry de Bracton**, *De Legibus et Consuetudinibus Angliae*; **Magna Carta** (1215). Bracton explicitly states that the king is under the law, and Magna Carta demonstrates rights as concrete protections ordered to justice and the common good.

[31] **Catechism of the Council of Trent**, Part III (Fourth Commandment; Sacraments); **St. Thomas Aquinas**, *Summa Theologiae*, II–II, q. 10, a. 12; q. 122. These sources affirm parental authority, the duty of provision, and the Church's right to worship without interference from temporal power.

[32] **Henry de Bracton**, *De Legibus et Consuetudinibus Angliae*, Book I; **St. Thomas Aquinas**, *Summa Theologiae*, I–II, q. 90, a. 3; q. 96, a. 4. Bracton famously

rights of his subjects was not merely illegal, but sinful.[33] Under this framework, the lower classes often enjoyed far more real freedoms than most people in the modern world can even imagine.[34]

Workers were organized into guilds, through which they regulated their own trades.[35] Guilds set wages, controlled prices, ensured quality, provided training, cared for widows and orphans, and protected members from exploitation by both nobles and merchants.[36] A shoemaker, baker, or mason did not

---

states that the king is under God and under the law, while Aquinas teaches that rulers are bound by law and that authority does not originate in personal will.

[33] **St. Thomas Aquinas**, *Summa Theologiae*, I–II, q. 92, a. 1; II–II, q. 42, a. 2; **Catechism of the Council of Trent**, Part III. Aquinas teaches that unjust rule and violations of justice are sins against both God and the common good, not merely legal infractions.

[34] **Alexis de Tocqueville**, *The Old Regime and the Revolution*; **Jean de Joinville**, *Life of Saint Louis*; **Magna Carta** (1215). These sources attest to the concrete liberties, legal protections, and lived freedoms exercised by common people under Christian monarchy and customary law.

[35] **Statutes of the Parisian Guilds**, compiled under **Étienne Boileau**, *Le Livre des Métiers* (c. 1268). This foundational text records the self regulation of trades in Paris, showing guild authority over labor, standards, and discipline.

[36] **Guild Statutes of Florence** (Arti Maggiori and Arti Minori); **Statutes of the Bakers' Guild of London**; **Statutes of the Cologne Guilds*. These statutes explicitly regulate wages, prices, apprenticeship, quality control, and charitable obligations toward members and their families.

answer to a distant corporation or a faceless bureaucracy, but to his own fraternity of craftsmen, governed by shared custom and mutual obligation.[37] Medieval cities such as Paris, Florence, Cologne, and London were prosperous precisely because economic life was local and ordered toward stability rather than endless growth.[38]

Education, charity, and welfare existed largely outside the state, provided through families, parishes, monasteries, and guilds.[39] The family was not isolated, atomized, or crushed under perpetual debt.[40] While material poverty certainly existed,

---

[37] **Bruno of Cologne**, *De Vita Solitaria* (on communal obligation); **Christopher Dyer**, *Standards of Living in the Later Middle Ages* (drawing on medieval records). Medieval sources and records demonstrate that craftsmen were governed locally by fraternities rooted in moral obligation rather than external administrative control.

[38] **Henri Pirenne**, *Medieval Cities*; **Jacques Le Goff**, *Time, Work, and Culture in the Middle Ages*. These works, based on medieval economic records, show that cities flourished through locally ordered economies aimed at continuity and social stability rather than unlimited expansion.

[39] **Rule of St. Benedict**, chs. 31–36; **Fourth Lateran Council** (1215), canons on parishes and education; **Guild Statutes of Paris and Florence**. These sources attest to education, charity, and welfare being administered through ecclesiastical, familial, and guild structures rather than centralized state authority.

[40] **St. Thomas Aquinas**, *Summa Theologiae*, II–II, q. 66, a. 2; **Pierre Bonnassie**, medieval manorial records (drawing on earlier charters). Aquinas affirms the moral

families were embedded in stable communities and protected from sudden dispossession.[41] Even serfs possessed enforceable rights to land, housing, and sustenance, even protection, and could not be arbitrarily evicted.[42] The medieval peasant was never at risk of losing everything because of a market fluctuation, a medical emergency, or a bureaucratic decree.[43]

Compare this to the modern family, which must submit either to corporate dependency or to state reliance simply to secure housing, food, education, and safety.[44] In democratic capitalism, work is

---

limits of property and debt, while medieval records show family stability and the absence of systemic debt dependence.

[41] **Marc Bloch**, *Feudal Society*; **Georges Duby**, *Rural Economy and Country Life in the Medieval West*. Based on medieval documents, these works show peasants embedded in stable communal structures with customary protections against sudden dispossession.

[42] **Manorial Court Rolls of England**; **Customs of Beauvaisis** (Philippe de Beaumanoir, c. 1283); **Henry de Bracton**, *De Legibus et Consuetudinibus Angliae*. These primary legal sources demonstrate that serfs had enforceable rights to land tenure, housing, and subsistence and could not be evicted arbitrarily.

[43] **Jean de Joinville**, *Life of Saint Louis*; **Statutes of Medieval Hospitals and Almshouses*. Contemporary accounts show that peasants relied on communal and ecclesiastical safety nets rather than volatile markets or bureaucratic systems.

[44] **U.S. Bureau of Labor Statistics**, *Historical Statistics of the United States, Colonial Times to 1957*; **U.S. Census Bureau**, *Housing and Home Finance* (1950).

increasingly insecure, debt is normalized, and families are uprooted in pursuit of employment.[45] In socialist systems, the same families are rendered dependent upon distant administrators and regulations.[46] In both cases, life is governed from above by systems too large and impersonal to be meaningfully resisted.[47]

The underlying difference is the principle of subsidiarity, long understood in Christian society; matters ought to be handled by the smallest, lowest, and most local authority capable of addressing

---

These reports document rising dependence on wage labor, mortgages, and institutional systems for basic necessities in the modern industrial economy.

45 **U.S. Bureau of Labor Statistics**, *Employment and Earnings Statistics* (1900–1957); **U.S. Census Bureau**, *Internal Migration in the United States, 1920–1950*. These reports show rising job instability, increased geographic mobility driven by employment necessity, and the normalization of household debt tied to wage dependence.

46 **Central Statistical Administration of the USSR**, *Statistical Yearbook of the Soviet Union* (1930s–1950s); **League of Nations**, *Economic Surveys of Europe* (interwar and postwar editions). These statistical publications document widespread state dependency for housing, employment, food distribution, and education under socialist administrative systems.

47 **League of Nations**, *Statistical Yearbook* (1926–1939); **United Nations**, *Statistical Yearbook* (1949–1957). Comparative data across industrial nations demonstrate the expansion of centralized administration, regulatory oversight, and institutional control over daily life, regardless of economic model.

them. In the Middle Ages, economic life was governed at the level of the workshop, the guild, the parish, and the town.[48] Today, nearly every aspect of life is subject to layers of regulation, licensing, taxation, and oversight imposed from far above.[49] What was once resolved by custom and neighborly authority now requires endless forms, permissions, and compliance.[50] The result is not freedom, but paralysis.[51]

---

[48] **Étienne Boileau**, *Le Livre des Métiers* (c. 1268); **Statutes of the Guilds of Florence*; **Town Charters of medieval France and the Holy Roman Empire*. These sources document that economic regulation was exercised locally through guilds, parishes, and municipal authority rather than centralized administration.

[49] **U.S. Bureau of Labor Statistics**, *Growth of Government Employment, 1900–1957*; **U.S. Census Bureau**, *Historical Statistics of the United States* (1957). These statistical records show the dramatic expansion of regulatory agencies, licensing regimes, and administrative oversight in modern industrial states.

[50] **League of Nations**, *Statistical Yearbook* (1926–1939); **International Labour Organization**, *Administrative Regulation of Industry* (1930s reports). These reports document the increase in procedural requirements, permits, and compliance mechanisms governing economic and social life.

[51] **Max Weber**, *Economy and Society* (based on pre-1920 research); **French Ministry of Finance**, *Statistiques Administratives* (interwar period); **OECD**, *Government at a Glance* (2011, 2015 editions). Weber's analysis and early twentieth-century administrative statistics document how bureaucratic expansion produces rigidity, delay, and loss of human agency. The OECD's twenty-first-century data confirms the same pattern, showing exponential growth in regulatory

While modern liberty is abstract, centralized, and conditional, medieval liberty was local, personal, and stable.[52] Modern citizens vote, but they do not govern.[53] Ironically, the lower classes in medieval Christendom often exercised more real influence over their conditions than any voter in a modern democracy, whose only participation is the occasional selection of rulers he will never meet and cannot meaningfully restrain.[54]

Of course, abuses of power existed among kings, lords, and all in positions of authority. The difference is that such abuses were legally,

---

bodies, compliance requirements, administrative staffing, and procedural complexity across modern democratic states, correlating with declining local autonomy and increasing institutional paralysis.

[52] **Magna Carta** (1215); **French Coutumes** (12th–14th c.); **St Thomas Aquinas**, *Summa Theologiae* I II q 90–97 on law and liberty.

[53] **Alexis de Tocqueville**, *Democracy in America* Book II ch 6–7., "*Testing Theories of American Politics: Elites, Interest Groups, and Average Citizens,*" *Perspectives on Politics*, Vol. 12, No. 3 (2014). Using thousands of policy outcomes in the United States, the authors demonstrate quantitatively that when the preferences of average citizens diverge from those of economic elites or organized interest groups, **the preferences of average citizens have near zero statistical impact on policy outcomes**. Policy change correlates strongly with elite and corporate preferences, not with voter majorities. By contrast, Medieval sources show **direct participation** through guilds, courts, parishes and customary law.

[54] **Town Charters of Laon Florence Cologne London**; **Manorial Court Rolls**, England 13th–15th c.

culturally, and morally restrained.[55] Under modern democracy, by contrast, corporate abuse is legal, often celebrated, and structurally protected, leading to the disenfranchisement of millions, particularly through the housing crisis.[56] Economic exploitation is not an aberration but systemic. Bureaucratic cruelty is not only procedural, but expected.[57] What once required moral justification now only requires regulatory compliance.

Famines and poverty occurred, but such misfortunes are inevitable in any society, regardless of its system. The difference lies not in the existence of scarcity, but in how it is handled. Parishes, guilds, monasteries, and nobles were bound by the moral teaching of the Church to feed the hungry and care for the poor. Many towns stored grain communally and regulated prices during shortages, ensuring that the cost of basic necessities would not be unjustly inflated.[58] Peasants could not be evicted from their

---

[55] **Canon Law Decretum Gratiani**; **Fourth Lateran Council** (1215); **Coronation Oaths of France and England**. **Martin Gilens and Benjamin I. Page**,

[56] **U.S. Census Bureau**, *Housing Vacancy and Homeownership Statistics*; **OECD**, *Housing Affordability* (2019).

[57] **ILO**, *Global Wage Report* (2018); **Piketty**, *Capital in the 21st Century*.

[58] **Rule of St Benedict** ch 31 53; **Parish Poor Rolls**; **Casti Connubii** principles of social obligation.

homes due to debt or unemployment.[59] Rather than relying on merchants or the state, communities relied on one another, facing hardship together rather than discarding individuals in times of need.[60] In the modern world, lavish mansions exist alongside tent cities, surplus food alongside starvation, and insulated wealthy communities alongside atomized lower classes.[61] To be poor in the Middle Ages was far more tolerable because the impoverished still possessed community and culture, and therefore access to basic necessities.[62] The modern poor, rather than simply being without abundance, are often without anything at all.[63]

The Middle Ages also carry a reputation for lacking upward mobility among the lower classes. This criticism stems from the modern assumption that upward mobility is a necessary condition for freedom. Modern man assumes that freedom means constant ascent, the ability to escape one's circumstances regardless of cost, and perpetual

---

[59] **Municipal Grain Statutes of Florence Siena Paris**; **Étienne Boileau**, *Livre des Métiers*.
[60] **English Manorial Customals**; **Bracton**, *De Legibus et Consuetudinibus Angliae*.
[61] **Guild Ordinances**; **Parish Records**; **Monastic Cartularies**.
[62] **FAO**, *Global Food Waste Index*; **UN Habitat**, *World Cities Report*.
[63] **Georges Duby**, *Rural Economy and Country Life*; **Eileen Power**, *Medieval People*.

change. While this appears attractive in theory, in practice it has not produced greater freedom for the lower classes.[64] Instead, nearly every aspect of human life, from luxury vacations to basic necessities, has been placed behind a paywall, regardless of whether the price demanded corresponds to any meaningful labor.[65] The uncomfortable truth is that a society which promises universal upward mobility usually delivers only universal insecurity.[66]

Medieval mobility, though limited, was real. Contrary to popular belief, it was both possible and frequent for those born into lower classes to rise. Apprentices became masters, peasants became landowners, and townsmen rose to positions of authority.[67] Clerics ascended regardless of birth, and noblemen could fall just as easily as they rose.[68] Even so, none of these groups lived under constant fear of losing their homes, families, or cultural roots.[69] Modern mobility, by contrast, is not merely optional but necessary just to survive, and it comes

---

[64] **World Bank**, *Poverty and Shared Prosperity* (2020).
[65] **Zygmunt Bauman**, *Liquid Modernity*.
[66] **Bureau of Labor Statistics**, *Household Expenditure Survey*.
[67] **OECD**, *Job Insecurity and Social Mobility* (2018).
[68] **Guild Apprenticeship Rolls**; **Urban Citizenship Records**.
[69] **Ecclesiastical Career Registers**; **Noble Attainders and Forfeitures**.

at a significant spiritual cost.[70] Families are uprooted, communities dissolved, and individuals locked into perpetual competition simply to get by.[71] This is not true freedom, but insecurity disguised as opportunity.

Medieval Christendom accepted human imperfection and built structures to restrain it. Modern systems deny human imperfection and therefore institutionalize it. Abuse is denied rather than restrained. Poverty is not shared but outsourced. Mobility is not merely offered but demanded. Medieval society limited power through structure. Modern society claims to limit power through theory. Structure works. Theory does not.

---

[70] **U.S. Census**, *Geographic Mobility Reports*.
[71] **Robert Nisbet**, *The Quest for Community*.

Chapter 3: "Monarchy Is Anti-Progress"

This claim stems from the assumption that progress is an absolute good, one which must be pursued regardless of circumstance or consequence.[72] The absurd additions to products made by technology companies in the 2020s, routinely passed off as "innovation," are evidence enough that this assumption is deeply flawed.[73] From the modernist perspective, progress is defined almost exclusively by the abstract, theoretical ability to do more.[74] One can earn money in countless ways. One can purchase food rather than produce it. One can perform tasks his ancestors never could through the advent of modern technology. Yet in burning the bridges of tradition, modern man has ensured that

---

[72] **José Ortega y Gasset**, *The Revolt of the Masses* (1930), esp. ch. 12–13, on progress treated as an unquestioned absolute rather than a moral good.

[73] **Lewis Mumford**, *Technics and Civilization* (1934), Even in 1934, there is documentation of the tendency of modern technological societies to mistake novelty for improvement.

[74] **Henri Bergson**, *Creative Evolution* (1907), critiquing purely quantitative notions of advancement divorced from human ends.

he possesses many poor choices rather than a few good ones.[75] The modernist philosophy naturally favors quantity over quality of choices, because to the modernist, quantity itself becomes the measure of quality.[76]

To the medieval mind, by contrast, progress was not defined by more options, but by the cultivation of tangible goods suited to the human person.[77] Innovation in the Middle Ages took the form of universities, hospitals, orphanages, Gothic architecture, legal systems, and enduring inventions that served real human needs.[78] This was not progress for its own sake, nor innovation detached from moral purpose, but progress ordered toward the betterment of man.[79] Such achievements were

---

[75] **G. K. Chesterton**, *The Outline of Sanity* (1926), on the loss of tradition producing multiplicity of options without genuine freedom.
[76] **Max Weber**, *The Protestant Ethic and the Spirit of Capitalism* (1905), on rationalization, efficiency, and quantity displacing substantive human goods.
[77] **St. Thomas Aquinas**, *Summa Theologiae*, I–II, q. 90–97, on law and human flourishing ordered to the common good rather than abstract choice.
[78] **Papal and Royal Charters of Medieval Universities** (Paris, Bologna, Oxford); **Rule of St. Benedict**, ch. 36; **Medieval hospital foundations** recorded in monastic cartularies.
[79] **St. Thomas Aquinas**, *De Regno*, Book I, on political order directed toward the virtuous life rather than material expansion. **Coronation Oaths of the Kings of France and England**; **Dom Prosper Guéranger**, *The*

possible precisely because feudal monarchy functioned as the guardian of culture, religion, and moral order, preserving what was good while allowing what was truly beneficial to grow.[80]

Liturgical Year, on the monarchy's role in preserving culture and moral order.

Part 2: Defining Monarchy

Chapter 4: Feudal Monarchy Versus Absolute Monarchy

Many in the West have been trained to think of all monarchy as absolute.[81] Whether it is imagined as the unchecked "control" of a king, or as the king's domination of the nobility and the Church. This misconception stems from the same modern error which insists that political agency can exist only through the vote.[82] Chapter Two of this book has already shown this assumption to be false. Nevertheless, absolute monarchy did exist in the West for a time, and it was genuinely oppressive.[83] Once the crown rejected the authority of the

---

[81] **Alexis de Tocqueville**, *Democracy in America*, Book II, ch. 1–6, on the modern tendency to conflate authority with centralized power and to view monarchy only through the lens of absolutism.

[82] **Jean-Jacques Rousseau**, *The Social Contract* (1762), Book I, ch. 6; contrasted with **St. Thomas Aquinas**, *Summa Theologiae* I–II, q. 90–97, on political authority not deriving from popular will alone.

[83] **Jacques-Bénigne Bossuet**, *Politics Drawn from the Very Words of Holy Scripture* (1709), illustrating the mature theory of absolute monarchy; contrasted with earlier medieval limits on royal authority.

Church, the restraints that had once limited royal power were removed, and the doors to abuse and corruption were thrown open.[84] Liberal-minded thinkers frequently criticize European monarchs and colonial ventures for their excesses, often failing, perhaps willfully, to recognize that these abuses arose not from *Catholic* monarchy, but from its abandonment.[85]

Critics of feudal monarchy may point out that such a system could not function without Catholicism. They would be correct.[86] Yet I would argue that any political system which rejects Christ's Church ultimately fails, regardless of how stable or effective it may appear on paper.[87] I intend to write another book defending the truth of the Catholic faith itself, but that is not the purpose of *this* work.

---

[84] **St. Thomas Aquinas**, *De Regno*, Book I; **Coronation Oaths of the Kings of France and England**, showing the king bound to divine and ecclesiastical law; **Act of Supremacy** (1534) as an example of the crown rejecting Church authority.

[85] **Pope Leo XIII**, *Aeterni Patris* (1879), on the abandonment of Thomistic political philosophy leading to modern political disorder; **Edmund Burke**, *Reflections on the Revolution in France* (1790).

[86] **Pope Pius XI**, *Quadragesimo Anno* (1931), on the necessity of Christian social order; **St. Robert Bellarmine**, *De Laicis*, on political authority presupposing the true religion.

[87] **St. Augustine**, *The City of God*, Book XIX, on political orders failing when separated from the true worship of God.

The argument presented here is more modest and more practical: that a feudal monarchy, even when merely governing *as though* Christ were King and the Catholic Church were His true Church, produces better political outcomes than its modern alternatives.[88] Before this can be demonstrated, however, a clear definition and distinction must be made between the feudal monarchies of the Middle Ages and the absolute monarchies that arose in the centuries leading up to the revolts against them.[89]

Feudal Monarchy

In medieval Europe, a king was not merely a ruler, but the steward of a nation. Authority was something he received, not something he seized for himself. Kingship was bound by Divine law, natural law, and long established custom. The crown was not a trophy or a reward, but a moral obligation.[90] A king held great wealth not for personal luxury, but because his position carried heavy public obligations. Since his wealth was largely inherited rather than earned through political maneuvering,

---

[88] **St. Thomas Aquinas**, *Summa Theologiae* I–II, q. 96, a. 4, on laws and regimes judged by their fruits in ordering society toward virtue and peace.

[89] **François Guizot**, *History of Civilization in Europe* (1828), Lectures 4–6, distinguishing medieval feudal monarchy from early modern absolutism and tracing the causes of revolutionary reaction.

he was expected to maintain the national court, support regional leaders, fund national defense, build and maintain infrastructure, provide charity, support religious institutions, and practice public generosity.[91] His status existed so that he could serve the Church above him and the people beneath him, and in return, they gave him their loyalty.[92]

Directly beneath the king were the high nobility: dukes, counts, and marquesses. These were regional governors who controlled large territories. In exchange for their land and status, they were responsible for local administration, public order, defense, and justice within their regions.[93] Just as importantly, if a king violated established law or abused those under his authority, these nobles could act together to oppose him, serving as a real and practical limit on centralized power.[94]

Below the high nobility were barons and knights. Barons functioned as local administrators, overseeing estates, presiding over courts, managing

---

[91] **Saint Thomas Aquinas**, *Summa Theologiae*, I–II, q. 90–97; De Regno, bk I, ch. 6

[92] **Capitulary of Charlemagne** (Capitulare de Villis); **Orderic Vitalis**, *Historia Ecclesiastica*

[93] **Rite of Coronation of the Kings of France** (Ordo ad consecrandum regem); **Hincmar of Reims**, *De Ordine Palatii*

[94] **Feudal Oaths of Homage**, collected in **Marc Bloch**, *Feudal Society*, vol. 1

disputes, and protecting the people who lived on their lands.[95] Knights served as local enforcers of law and order and as trained soldiers when defense was required. Their authority was tied directly to service. Honor and virtue were essential to their role, and a knight who abused power was seen as a failure, not a success.[96]

Not everyone lived under a lord. There were free men and townspeople who answered directly to the king. This group included merchants, craftsmen, artisans, and professionals. They governed themselves through town councils, local courts, and guilds.[97] Guilds were not merely trade organizations. They were economic and political institutions which enforced standards of morality.[98] They regulated trades, set standards of quality, trained apprentices, supported members and their families, disciplined misconduct, and protected workers from exploitation.[99] Economic life was local, personal, and ordered toward stability rather than constant expansion.[100]

---

95 **Magna Carta** (1215); **Matthew Paris**, *Chronica Majora*

96 **Assizes of Jerusalem**; **Beaumanoir**, *Coutumes de Beauvaisis*

97 **Geoffroi de Charny**, *Book of Chivalry*

98 Town Charters of Laon, Lübeck, and Florence

99 **Statutes of the Paris Guilds** (Livre des métiers, Étienne Boileau)

100 **Henri Pirenne**, *Medieval Cities*

At the base of society were peasants and serfs, who made up most of the population. Peasants were producers, working family plots and shared land. Their obligations were fixed and predictable, usually consisting of a set number of workdays per week, rents paid in goods or money, and seasonal services.[101] This predictability made their lives economically stable, even if modest. Serfdom, contrary to popular belief, was not slavery but a legal status. Serfs were tied to the land, not owned by a person. They could not be sold on their own, could not be removed from their homes without serious cause, and had legal standing in local courts.[102] They often passed land down to their children and could formally challenge abusive lords.[103] While abuse did occur, it was usually restrained, since cruelty risked legal punishment, religious sanction, collective resistance, or intervention by higher authority.[104]

While imperfect, society under this system flourished. Authority was decentralized, which allowed ordinary people to exercise real control over their work, communities, and daily lives.[105]

---

[101] **Manorial Rolls of England and France**, 12th–14th centuries

[102] **Bracton**, *De Legibus et Consuetudinibus Angliae*

[103] Court Rolls of the Manor of Wakefield

[104] **Council of Lateran IV** (1215); **Gratian**, *Decretum*

[105] **Marc Bloch**, *Feudal Society*, Vol. I (1939), especially Part II, chapters 1–3.

One might ask, then, if this system functioned so well, why it dissolved over the following centuries. How did we arrive at our present condition? Feudal monarchy did not collapse all at once, but was gradually weakened by prolonged warfare, demographic shocks, monetary change, and the deliberate centralization of power.

Absolute Monarchy, and How Kingship Was Transformed from Stewardship into Domination

The transition from feudal monarchy to absolute monarchy in Europe took place over roughly two to three centuries, and it was not inevitable.[106] Beginning in the fifteenth century, ruling families such as the Tudors and the Habsburgs, and later figures like Louis XIV, slowly set aside the restraints once imposed by the Church and by

---

Bloch explicitly describes feudal society as characterized by dispersed authority, local custom, and reciprocal obligations, noting that political and economic power was exercised primarily at the local level through lords, guilds, villages, and courts, rather than through a centralized state. He emphasizes that this decentralization gave ordinary people stability, participation, and protection within their immediate social structures.
106

feudal custom.[107] Power became more centralized in the hands of the state.[108] Medieval institutions continued to exist in name, but their real authority was steadily weakened or deliberately dismantled.[109] What followed was not the fulfillment of monarchy, but its corruption.[110]

The collapse of healthy kingship did not begin simply with wicked rulers, but with the rejection of God.[111] In medieval Christendom, the Church stood above all as the highest moral authority in society.[112] The Church did not rule kingdoms directly, but judged rulers by a higher law than their own.[113] Through teaching, preaching, canon law, and sacramental discipline, the Church reminded all men that authority came from God and existed for

---

[107] Marc Bloch, *Feudal Society*, Vol. II, especially chapters on decentralization of authority and reciprocal obligations between estates.

[108] G. R. Elton, *The Tudor Revolution in Government,* detailing the administrative centralization under Henry VIII and his successors.

[109] Max Weber, *Economy and Society* Part I, ch. 3, on rational legal authority and state centralization.

[110] Otto Hintze, "The Preconditions of Representative Government" in *State and Constitution* (original essays early 20th c.).

[111] Jacques Maritain, *Man and the State* on the corruption of authority when detached from natural and divine law.

[112] Augustine, *City of God*, Book XIX, on political order collapsing when divorced from God.

[113] Pope Gelasius I, *Duo Sunt* (494 AD,) articulating the doctrine of the two powers, sacred and royal.

the common good.[114] Excommunication, interdict, and ecclesiastical courts were not symbolic gestures.[115] They were real limits on power.[116] A king who stood outside the Church stood outside true legitimacy.[117]

This authority depended not only on institutions, but on holiness and credibility.[118] Over time, these foundations weakened. Corruption arose within the clergy.[119] Some bishops became too involved in court politics, neglected their pastoral duties, or sought wealth and influence rather than holiness. Church offices were sometimes treated as privileges, and discipline was applied unevenly.[120] While the Church always possessed the means to correct these problems, their persistence in secular

---

[114] Gratian, *Decretum*, Distinction X and XI, on the supremacy of divine and natural law over rulers.
[115] Thomas Aquinas, *Summa Theologiae*, I–II, Q.90–97 on law, authority, and the common good.
[116] Gregory VII, *Dictatus Papae*, asserting real ecclesiastical limits on secular rulers.
[117] Eamon Duffy, *Saints and Sinners*, sections on medieval papal authority and discipline.
[118] Innocent III, *Venerabilem*, on papal authority in judging imperial legitimacy.
[119] St. Bernard of Clairvaux, *De Consideratione*, addressed to Pope Eugene III, on moral authority grounded in holiness rather than office alone.
[120] Fourth Lateran Council (1215) canons addressing clerical reform and discipline.

matters weakened her credibility in the eyes of rulers and ordinary people alike.[121]

A corrupt cleric may still hold legal authority, but he struggles to command moral authority.[122] When clergy failed to live as spiritual fathers, kings found it easier to dismiss Church restraint as hypocrisy or self interest rather than obedience to divine law.[123] For good clerics to exist, they must usually be raised by faithful Catholic families.[124] When this foundation weakened, the priesthood suffered. In many places, clerical life became less a calling freely embraced and more a role imposed for political or economic reasons.[125] Younger sons of noble families were sometimes pushed into monasteries or bishoprics for convenience, not vocation.[126] Others entered the clergy for income, status, or security.[127] A man who enters holy orders

---

[121] John of Salisbury, *Policraticus* Books IV–V, critiquing clerical worldliness and political entanglement.
[122] Council of Trent, Session XXV on reform of ecclesiastical offices and discipline.
[123] R. W. Southern, *Western Society and the Church*, chapters on clerical authority and decline.
[124] Aquinas, *Commentary on Aristotle's Politics* Book III, on moral legitimacy versus legal authority.
[125] Luther, *Address to the Christian Nobility* used here as evidence of how clerical corruption was rhetorically exploited.
[126] Catechism of the Council of Trent, *Session XXIII* (15 July 1563),
[127] Georges Duby, *The Three Orders*, on social roles and clerical placement.

for worldly reasons may wear the vestments, but he will rarely live the calling.

At the same time, the laity began to take the Faith for granted.[128] Christendom had existed for so long that many assumed it would continue without effort or vigilance. Parents no longer saw themselves as the first teachers of faith and morals. Fewer demanded holiness from their priests.[129] Fewer resisted scandal when it appeared. The Faith was inherited as culture, but no longer practiced with seriousness.[130]

When poorly formed clergy and spiritually complacent laity combined, corruption was no longer corrected early. Instead, it was tolerated or ignored.[131] Over time, this produced a priesthood lacking zeal and a people less willing to defend the Church when she disciplined kings or lords.[132] When laymen excused immoral clergy or sided with powerful rulers against ecclesiastical authority, they weakened the very institution meant to protect

---

[128] Council of Basel records, decrees and debates on benefices and clerical abuses.

[129] Canon Law, Gratian, on parental responsibility in moral formation.

[130] Johan Huizinga, *The Waning of the Middle Ages*, on spiritual complacency in late medieval society.

[131] Episcopal visitation records from France and England, 14th–15th centuries..

[132] Council of Constance (1414–1418), reform decrees.

them.[133] A people unwilling to defend the Church against corruption eventually became unable to defend her against open attack.[134] When rulers later assaulted ecclesiastical authority, many welcomed it, mistaking the removal of restraint for the removal of abuse itself.[135] What was lost was not merely bad clergy, but the living bond between shepherd and flock that had once sustained Christendom.

With the Church removed as a real restraint, nothing remained above the crown. Law ceased to be something the king obeyed and became something he issued.[136] Power no longer required moral justification, only legal enforcement.[137]

What followed was not liberation for any class, but harm to all of them. Each social group lost something essential, and in losing its proper place, society lost balance.[138] What had once been a

---

133 **Eamon Duffy**, *Saints and Sinners.*
134 **R. W. Southern**, *Western Society and the Church.*
135 **John Wycliffe**, *De Ecclesia*, illustrating lay alignment against ecclesiastical authority.
136 **Georges Duby**, *The Three Orders.* See also **Henry VIII**, *Act of Supremacy* (1534).
137 **Jean Bodin**, *Les Six Livres de la République* (*Six Books of the Commonwealth*), defining sovereignty as absolute.
138 **Thomas Hobbes**, *Leviathan*, chs. 18–26.

hierarchy of mutual obligation became a system of domination from above.[139]

Under feudal monarchy, dukes and counts governed regions. They were responsible for justice, defense, and order.[140] Their authority was local, real, and rooted in custom. As absolutism rose, this authority was deliberately stripped away. Nobles were drawn into royal courts, kept dependent on royal favor, deprived of independent military power, and replaced in governance by royal ministers and bureaucrats.[141] They became ornaments of the crown rather than leaders of men. With their fall, no strong intermediary remained between the king and the people.[142]

The lower nobility and knights lost their purpose. As standing armies replaced feudal levies and centralized courts replaced local justice, knights were no longer needed. Many became poor or irrelevant.[143] Communities lost personal protection, and the use of force became the monopoly of the state rather than a shared responsibility.[144]

---

[139] **Alexis de Tocqueville**, *L'Ancien Régime et la Révolution*.
[140] Ibid.
[141] Medieval customary law codes (e.g., *Coutumes de Beauvaisis*).
[142] **G. R. Elton**, *The Tudor Revolution in Government*.
[143] **Norbert Elias**, *The Court Society*.
[144] **Tocqueville**, *The Old Regime and the Revolution*.

Free men and townspeople had once governed themselves through local institutions, but as absolutism expanded, these liberties were steadily reduced.[145] Active participation in public life became passive obedience. Citizenship was reduced to compliance.[146]

Guilds suffered especially severe losses.[147] They once regulated wages, prices, training, quality of goods, working conditions, and care for families.[148] Absolutist states saw guilds as obstacles to central control. As a result, they were restricted, absorbed, or abolished.[149] Without guilds, workers lost protection, labor lost dignity, skill was subordinated to profit, and economic life became competitive and unstable.[150] This prepared the ground for later industrial exploitation.[151]

Peasants and serfs lost their protections as well. Customary rights to land weakened.[152] Taxes

---

145 **Maurice Keen**, *Chivalry.*
146 **Geoffrey Parker**, *The Military Revolution.*
147 **Keen**, *Chivalry.*
148 **Max Weber**, *Economy and Society.*
149 Medieval city charters of Florence, London, Cologne.
150 **Tocqueville**, *The Old Regime.*
151 **Weber**, *Economy and Society.*
152 Guild statutes of Paris, Florence, and London (12th–15th c.).

increased.[153] Rents were monetized.[154] Enclosure expanded.[155] Where peasants once had secure land, predictable duties, and community support, they now faced debt, displacement, and exposure to market forces.[156] They gained abstract freedom, but lost real security. In the misery that followed this corrupted form of monarchy, it is no surprise that people later turned against it.

When I said earlier that life functioned better when society acted as though Christ were King and the Church had real authority, this is what I meant; medieval peasants were poorer and more limited, yet in many ways more free.[157] By the time the revolutions came, monarchy no longer resembled its earlier form. The people did not revolt against feudal kingship.[158] They revolted against unchecked power, distant authority, arbitrary law, and economic insecurity. Each class suffered not because hierarchy existed, but because its proper structure had been destroyed.

---

[153] **Jean-Baptiste Colbert**, royal ordinances.
[154] French revolutionary decrees abolishing guilds (1791).
[155] **Karl Polanyi**, *The Great Transformation.*
[156] **Friedrich Engels**, *The Condition of the Working Class in England.*
[157] Brenner Debate historical economic sources.
[158] **Polanyi**, *The Great Transformation.*

Instead of calling for the restoration of the Catholic state, people turned to democratic systems.[159] Renaissance and Enlightenment thinkers emphasized reason, choice, and popular sovereignty. These ideas offered an explanation for resisting kings and promised a system where authority came from consent rather than birth.[160] To those living under arbitrary rule, democracy appeared to offer accountability in a world where traditional checks had failed.

The people did not demand a return to feudal monarchy because the institutions that made it work had already been destroyed.[161] By then, hierarchy was understood only as oppression.[162] Democracy was presented as liberation, even though it replaced concrete structures with abstract promises.[163] Democracy was chosen not because it was better, but because the institutions that could have supported a just Catholic monarchy had been discredited or erased.[164] The people did not revolt

---

159 **Bloch**, *Feudal Society.*
160 **Tocqueville**, *The Old Regime.*
161 **John Locke**, *Second Treatise of Government.*
162 **Jean-Jacques Rousseau**, *The Social Contract.*
163 **Thomas Paine**, *Common Sense.*
164 **Alexis de Tocqueville**, *The Old Regime and the Revolution*, Part I, chs. 1–4, where Tocqueville explains that the destruction of intermediary institutions made reform impossible and left revolution as the only perceived alternative.

against monarchy itself, but against unrestrained and corrupted monarchy.[165] In that vacuum, democracy seemed like the only option.[166]

---

[165] **The Federalist Papers**, especially Nos. 1, 9, and 10, which frame rebellion as resistance to abuse of power rather than to authority itself, and argue that unchecked power provokes popular revolt.

[166] **Max Weber**, *Economy and Society*, Part I, ch. 3, on the collapse of traditional authority and the turn toward rational-legal legitimacy as a replacement.

Karl Polanyi, *The Great Transformation*, chs. 3–6, describing how the dismantling of older social institutions forced societies into abstract political and economic systems perceived as the only viable alternatives.

Alexis de Tocqueville, *The Old Regime and the Revolution*, Part III, showing how centralized absolutism left no path but democratic revolution once legitimacy collapsed.

Chapter 5: Organic Versus Artificial Society

Modern people have been raised to believe that a functioning society is built on individuals pursuing their own desires. In reality, society is built on relationships. The family unit demonstrates this plainly: the bonds of husband and wife, father and child, mother and child, and between siblings all form the backbone of civilization.[167] As noted earlier, the failure of parents to properly raise their children contributed to the emergence of poorly formed clergy and the subsequent weakening of the Church's authority.[168] If parents neglect their responsibilities, children will not develop into decent adults. Society depends on the formation of virtuous people; without them, no structure or order

---

[167] **St. Thomas Aquinas**, *Summa Theologica*, II-II, Q. 57, a. 1–2: Discusses the moral duties of parents in guiding and forming children, highlighting the family as the fundamental unit of social and moral order.

[168] **Council of Trent (1545–1563)**, Session V, "On the Sacrament of Confirmation and the duty of Christian instruction": Emphasizes the role of parents in raising children in the faith, linking family education to the health of the Church and society.

can endure.[169] For those wondering how America, once a prosperous nation, could decline so rapidly within a few decades, this is the primary reason.

Medieval society understood this, at least for a time. The peoples of each nation under feudal monarchy functioned like organisms, with distinct yet harmonious members. Human beings were not merely isolated individuals, yet not fully absorbed into a collective either. Persons are always related to one another, yet remain distinct and unique.[170]

Self-Governing Communities Versus Individuals in Bureaucracy

Under feudal monarchy, society was not organized around the isolated individual, but around a network of natural and inherited communities: the family, the parish, the guild, the crown. Authority flowed downward through these institutions rather than

---

[169] **St. Augustine**, *The City of God,* Book XIX, ch. 16: Notes that the maintenance of society depends on the moral formation of its citizens; vice in private life inevitably produces disorder in the public realm. **Note also** the famous quote made by John Adams in his letter to the Massachusetts Militia in 1798: *"Our Constitution was made only for a moral and religious People. It is wholly inadequate to the government of any other."*

[170] **Aristotle**, *Politics*, Book I, ch. 2: Notes that humans are by nature political animals, forming communities in which distinct individuals contribute to a harmonious whole.

outward from a distant center.[171] The king stood not as a manager of daily life, but as the guardian of order and continuity.[172] Most of what governed a person's life occurred far below the level of the crown, within structures he knew personally and could meaningfully influence.[173]

This stands in sharp contrast to the modern state, in which authority is centralized and abstract.[174] Today, families, parishes, and local communities exist largely at the mercy of national bureaucracies and economic forces beyond their control.[175] Under feudal monarchy, these smaller bodies were not obstacles to governance, but the very means by

---

[171] **St. Thomas Aquinas**, *Summa Theologiae*, I–II, q.90, a.2; II–II, q.58, a.1–2, where law and justice are ordered to the common good through natural social units rather than isolated individuals.
[172] **Philippe de Beaumanoir**, *Coutumes de Beauvaisis* (c. 1283), prologue and Book I, describing customary law exercised locally through families, villages, and lordships rather than centralized authority.
[173] **John of Salisbury**, *Policraticus* (1159), Book IV, where the king is described as the guardian and servant of the political body, not its master.
[174] *Magna Carta* (1215), especially clauses 13, 39, and 40, affirming local liberties, customary rights, and legal processes exercised close to the people.
[175] **Alexis de Tocqueville**, Democracy in America (1835), Vol. I, Part II, ch. 5–6, on the tendency of modern states toward administrative centralization and abstraction.

which governance occurred.[176] Modern society, in its prioritization of individual freedom and personal distinction above all other goods, ironically treats persons as cogs in a machine: all while simultaneously praising them for being "unique" and "special."[177]

Economic life for medievalists was likewise structured around stability rather than growth or competition.[178] Guilds gave workers real authority over their trades. Craftsmen did not merely sell their labor; they governed it.[179] Wages, prices, training, quality standards, and working conditions were all regulated by those who actually practiced the trade.[180] This gave artisans dignity, security, and a direct voice in their economic lives that modern

---

[176] **Pope Leo XIII**, Rerum Novarum (1891), §§35–36, condemning the absorption of family and local functions by centralized authority and St. Thomas Aquinas, De Regno, Book I, ch. 2–3, on governance proceeding through ordered parts of society, with the ruler coordinating rather than replacing lower authorities.
[177] **Pope Leo XIII**, *Rerum Novarum* (1891), no. 11–12: Critiques the reduction of persons to labor units in economic systems that ignore moral and social bonds.
[178] Marc Bloch, *La Société Féodale* (1939), Vol. I, Part II, ch. 2.
[179] Statutes of the Parisian Guilds, compiled under Étienne Boileau, *Livre des Métiers* (c. 1268).
[180] Ibid.; see also Georges Renard, *Guilds in the Middle Ages* (English trans. 1918).

workers, subject to corporate policy or state regulation, rarely possess.[181]

Crucially, obligations throughout society were customary and predictable.[182] Lords could not arbitrarily raise rents or labor demands. Peasants knew what was owed of them and what they were owed in return.[183] This predictability allowed families to plan, to save, and to live without constant fear of sudden dispossession. Peasants retained sufficient time for their own subsistence, community obligations, and religious life.[184] While their material conditions were modest, they were economically stable, a condition increasingly rare in the modern world.

Peasant life was deeply communal and rooted.[185] Most people lived within villages, parishes, and extended kin networks that endured for generations. Life revolved around the agricultural calendar, feast

---

[181] **Wilhelm Roscher,** *Political Economy*, Book III, ch. 4 (19th c. historian drawing on medieval sources).
[182] Beaumanoir, *Coutumes de Beauvaisis* (c. 1283), esp. chs. 24–30.
[183] **Ibid**.; also English Manorial Court Rolls, e.g., *Select Pleas in Manorial Courts*, Selden Society.
[184] **Dom Prosper Guéranger**, *L'Année Liturgique*; corroborated by agrarian calendars in medieval breviaries.
[185] **Marc Bloch**, *French Rural History* (1931).

days, shared labor, and the Church year.[186] Work, worship, and leisure were not sharply divided but integrated into a coherent way of life. Individuals were not treated as isolated economic units, but as members of a living community.[187]

These interconnected social structures provided what neither markets nor states can easily supply: mutual aid, shared tools, communal decision making, and moral accountability.[188] When hardship came, it was faced together. When disputes arose, they were settled locally, by people who understood the context and the individuals involved.[189]

Taxation As Necessity Versus Taxation As Theft

Under feudal monarchy, the financial foundation of government differed radically from that of the modern state.[190] Because the king's wealth was primarily inherited rather than extracted, he could

---

[186] Breviarium Romanum; see also Eamon Duffy, *The Stripping of the Altars* (drawing on pre-Reformation parish records).
[187] St. Thomas Aquinas, *Summa Theologiae*, I–II, q. 90–97 (law ordered to the common good).
[188] Alexis de Tocqueville, *The Old Regime and the Revolution*, Book I, ch. 2 (on intermediary bodies).
[189] English and French manorial court records; see also Frederic Seebohm, *The English Village Community* (1883).
[190] Marc Bloch, *Feudal Society*, Vol. I, Part II, ch. 1.

fund public obligations without imposing crushing burdens on the population. Royal revenues came chiefly from crown lands, feudal dues, tolls, and long established customary rights, not from the constant expansion of taxation.[191] The crown was, in effect, a landed household with public responsibilities. This arrangement naturally limited both the size and the reach of government, since the king could spend only what his estates and customary incomes produced.[192]

Taxes under this system were not the default means of governance, but an extraordinary measure.[193] They were typically levied for specific and temporary purposes such as war, ransom, or emergency relief, and often required the consent of estates, councils, or assemblies. Because taxation was visible, limited, and exceptional, it was politically dangerous to abuse.[194] A king who taxed excessively risked resistance from the nobility, refusal from towns, or condemnation from the

---

191 F. W. Maitland, *The Constitutional History of England* (1908), lectures on royal revenue.
192 Joseph Strayer, *On the Medieval Origins of the Modern State* (1970), ch. 2 (describing limits of medieval royal finance).
193 Magna Carta (1215), clauses 12 and 14.
194 Philippe de Beaumanoir, *Coutumes de Beauvaisis* (c. 1283).

Church. In this sense, taxation functioned as a last resort, not as the lifeblood of the state.[195]

By contrast, the modern government possesses no inherited wealth of its own. It owns little that generates independent revenue and therefore must extract wealth directly from the people to sustain itself.[196] Every public program, however well intentioned, is funded not by surplus held by the state, but by compulsory transfer from private citizens. What is presented as "public spending" is, in practice, legalized expropriation.[197] The phrase "taxation is theft," under this system, is accurate, and widely popular for this reason. The modern state cannot give without first taking, and it cannot expand without first extracting more.[198]

This difference has profound consequences. Because modern governments depend entirely on taxation, they are structurally incentivized to grow.[199] Bureaucracies must justify their existence, budgets must increase, and new programs must be

---

[195] **John of Salisbury**, *Policraticus*, Book IV.
[196] **OECD**, *Revenue Statistics 2023* (showing tax dependence of modern states).
[197] **Murray Rothbard**, *Power and Market* (drawing on classical definitions of taxation).
[198] **U.S. Congressional Budget Office**, *Historical Budget Data*.
[199] **Max Weber**, *Economy and Society*, Part III (bureaucratic expansion).

created to secure political loyalty. Taxation becomes permanent, diffuse, and opaque, spread across income, consumption, property, inheritance, and inflation.[200] Unlike medieval taxes, which were debated and resisted, modern taxation is normalized and largely unavoidable.

Paradoxically, the king's inherited wealth also served as a shield against corruption.[201] He did not need to campaign for office, purchase loyalty, or enrich himself after attaining power. He had no donors to appease and no electoral base to flatter. His material interests were already secured, and his incentive lay not in accumulation, but in preservation.[202] A king who squandered his patrimony weakened not only himself, but his heirs and his dynasty.

Modern rulers, by contrast, enter office without wealth attached to their position and exit it with every incentive to capitalize on their power while they can.[203] They must raise funds, court donors, promise benefits, and secure post office opportunities. Corruption is not an aberration in such a system; it is a predictable outcome. Power is

---

200 **OECD**, *Tax Policy Reforms 2022.*
201 **St. Thomas Aquinas,** *Summa Theologiae*, II–II, q. 61 (on justice and rulers).
202 **Ernst Kantorowicz**, *The King's Two Bodies* (1957), on dynastic responsibility.
203 **James Burnham,** *The Machiavellians* (1943).

temporary, but access to wealth *through* power is immediate.[204]

Under monarchy, taxation existed, but it was restrained by custom, consent, and necessity.[205] Under modern government, taxation is the foundation of rule itself. The medieval king governed with what he had. The modern state governs by taking what others have.[206] The former made restraint possible. The latter makes exploitation inevitable.

The Role of Women in Society

The role of women within this system further exposes the difference between true and false freedom.[207] Medieval society did not promise women liberation through abstraction or ideological slogans. Instead, it recognized concrete goods: motherhood, household authority, communal respect, and meaningful participation in economic and social life.[208] A woman's labor within the home,

---

204 **Transparency International**, *Global Corruption Report*.

205 *Council of Lateran IV* (1215), canons on just taxation and ecclesiastical consent.

206 **Alexis de Tocqueville**, *The Old Regime and the Revolution*, Book I.

207 **St. Thomas Aquinas**, *Summa Theologiae*, II–II, q. 57–58 (justice ordered to real goods).

208 **Georges Duby**, *Women of the Twelfth Century* (1997, drawing on medieval sources).

the village, and often the guild was not invisible or sentimentalized, but socially necessary and economically real. She was not forced to choose between family and survival, nor told that fulfillment required imitation of masculine patterns of life.[209]

The modern fixation on voting as the sole expression of agency has deeply distorted how freedom itself is understood.[210] This assumption that authority can only be exercised through direct participation in the upper classes of society did not stop with the fall of monarchy. It bled into every sphere of life, including the feminist movement. First the authority of the Church was rejected, then the authority of the king, then the nobility, then the employer with the rise of Marxism, and finally the natural authority of man within the family.[211] Each layer of order was stripped away in the name of liberation, leaving only the isolated individual facing an ever expanding state.

G. K. Chesterton saw this clearly when he addressed women's suffrage.[212] He did not oppose

---

[209] **Philippe de Beaumanoir**, *Coutumes de Beauvaisis* (c. 1283).
[210] **Alexis de Tocqueville**, *Democracy in America*, Vol. I.
[211] **Pope Leo XIII**, *Rerum Novarum* (1891), sections on authority and social order.
[212] **G. K. Chesterton**, *What's Wrong with the World* (1910)

women's dignity, nor deny their intelligence or moral seriousness. He argued that the vote, in a centralized mass democracy, was a weak substitute for the real authority women already exercised within the family and the local community.[213] A woman who governs a household, shapes the moral imagination of children, and participates in a living neighborhood possesses far more real power than a woman reduced to casting a ballot once every few years for rulers she will never meet and cannot restrain. The tragedy, Chesterton observed, was not that women gained the vote, but that they were offered the vote as compensation for the loss of everything else.[214]

The world consistently falls into one of two errors regarding women. Either women are treated as beneath men, as lesser or even subhuman, or they are treated as interchangeable with men, equal in the false sense that difference itself must be denied.[215] The Catholic answer rejects both. Women possess the same dignity as men, because both are made in the image of God.[216] Yet they are not equal in the sense of being identical or interchangeable. A

---

[213] **Ibid.**, ch. 4 "Feminism, or the Mistake About Woman."
[214] **G. K. Chesterton**, *The Thing* (1929), essays on suffrage and local authority.
[215] **Pope Pius XI**, *Casti Connubii* (1930).
[216] Genesis 1:27; Council of Trent, Catechism, section on marriage.

child has the same dignity as an adult, yet no one claims a seven year old is equal in authority or responsibility to a grown man. A pilot and a firefighter have equal dignity, but they do not perform the same role. A neurosurgeon and a chef, a tall man and a short man, may each contribute something essential, without being reducible to one another. Difference does not imply inferiority. It implies a difference in purpose.[217]

Unlike pagan societies that treated women as property, or modern secular societies that treat them as economic units, medieval society integrated women into social life in ways that were complementary rather than competitive.[218] Women held authority within households, managed estates, participated in guild economies, inherited property, ruled as regents or queens, and exercised influence through parish and communal life. Widows were not discarded, but rather often possessed legal autonomy.[219] Women who did not fit neatly into the role of wife or mother found places in religious life, craft production, education, and charity. Arguably, the spread of Christendom was the greatest single

---

217 **St. Thomas Aquinas**, *Summa Theologiae*, I, q. 47 (order and diversity).

218 **Régine Pernoud**, *Those Terrible Middle Ages!* (1977, medieval documentation).

219 English Common Law, widow's dower rights; see Maitland, *History of English Law*.

improvement in the condition of women in human history precisely because it rejected both domination and erasure.[220]

Raising children under this system was not an isolating task, but a shared one. Society itself was structured to support motherhood. Communities were stable and walkable. Extended family lived nearby. Parishes, feast days, and shared labor wove daily life together.[221] Trust was high and children belonged not only to parents but to a culture that reinforced what parents taught. Women were not meant to raise children alone, cut off from kin, community, and meaning. They are social creatures because childrearing is a social task.[222]

The collapse of feudal society and the rise of industrialization destroyed these supports.[223] Work was pulled out of the home. Men were separated from family life for long hours. Women were left alone with children in isolated dwellings, cut off from extended family and meaningful communal life. It is no wonder that motherhood began to feel overwhelming, exhausting, and even imprisoning. Feminism did not arise primarily because women

---

[220] **Régine Pernoud**, *Women in the Middle Ages* (1962).
[221] **Dom Prosper Guéranger**, *The Liturgical Year.*
[222] **Aristotle**, *Politics*, Book I (household as social foundation), received through Scholastic tradition.
[223] **Wilhelm Heinrich Riehl**, *The Natural History of the German People* (1855).

hated children or rejected family, but because women were abandoned by society and told to endure the consequences alone.[224]

Feminism promises freedom through independence from obligation, yet merely replaces it with dependence on employers, markets, or the state. Medieval monarchy, by contrast, offered women a freedom rooted in protection, stability, and social recognition.[225] It did not deny difference. It ordered difference toward the common good. Where modern systems isolate women in the name of "autonomy," Christendom integrated them in the name of charity, duty, and shared life.[226]

---

224 **Pope Pius XI**, *Quadragesimo Anno* (1931), on industrial disruption of family life.
225 **Leo XIII**, *Arcanum Divinae Sapientiae* (1880).
226 **St. Robert Bellarmine**, *De Laicis*, Book III.

Part 3: Monarchy Versus Modern Ideologies

Chapter 6: The King as Political Father of the Nation

A political system is a philosophy applied to reality. By this, I mean that every political system is built upon an idea of what man is and how he ought to live. Government does not merely manage power; it expresses an ideology about human nature. This is why the claim that religion and government ought to "be separated" is not only unrealistic, but arguably impossible. Religion answers the question of man's purpose, while politics concerns how men ought to govern themselves. The latter will always be informed by what governing bodies believe the former to be.

While the modern state often behaves as though man's purpose is to labor endlessly for material goods he will scarcely enjoy, Christendom understood that man's end is beatitude. The goods of this life are meant to form man for the next life. The material world ought to serve man, not the other way around.

Saint Thomas Aquinas emphasizes in his work, *De Regimine Principum*, that political authority exists not to serve wealth or material accumulation, but to promote the moral and spiritual good of the people.[227] He repeatedly stresses that rulers are bound to govern in a way that directs their subjects toward virtue and ultimately eternal union with God rather than mere temporal prosperity.[228] Those in authority bear it for those beneath him, not the other way around.[229]

In the medieval mind, politics was understood as ordered toward man's true end, beatitude. Thus, kingship was understood in paternal terms.[230] If man is not made merely for production, consumption, or self expression, but for beatitude, then political authority cannot exist simply to maximize output or

---

[227] **St. Thomas Aquinas**, *De Regno ad Regem Cypri* (also known as *De Regimine Principum*), Book I, ch. 1–3, where Aquinas argues that the end of political rule is the common good, not private gain or wealth accumulation.

[228] **St. Thomas Aquinas**, *De Regno*, Book I, ch. 14–15; see also *Summa Theologiae*, I–II, q. 90, a. 2, where law and governance are explicitly ordered toward virtue and man's final end, not merely material well-being.

[229] **St. Thomas Aquinas**, *Summa Theologiae*, II–II, q. 42, a. 2; cf. **Gregory the Great**, *Regula Pastoralis*, Book I, ch. 2, a foundational text Aquinas inherits, which teaches that authority is exercised for the benefit of subjects, not the ruler.

[230] **St. Thomas Aquinas**, *De Regno*, I, ch. 1–2 (on man's final end and the ordering of political authority).

manage competing interests. It must exist to guide, protect, and order society toward the conditions in which souls can flourish. This is precisely the role of a father.[231]

A father does not govern his household by contract, ideology, or abstraction. He governs by responsibility. His authority is not self chosen, nor granted by vote, but received with the burden of care. He is answerable not only for outcomes, but for persons. Medieval Christendom applied this same logic to the king. The king was not conceived as a manager of resources or a representative of popular will, but as the head of a political household, responsible for the moral and material well being of his people across generations.[232]

Because man's ultimate end was understood to be beatitude, the king's task was necessarily limited. He was not meant to remake human nature, engineer equality, or promise happiness in this world. Like a father, the king was expected to rule with restraint, patience, and continuity, knowing

---

[231] **Aristotle**, *Politics*, Book I; received and developed in the Scholastic tradition.

[232] **John of Salisbury**, *Policraticus*, Book IV (the ruler as head of the political body, analogous to household governance).

that abuse of power harmed not only his subjects, but his own soul and the inheritance of his heirs.[233]

The medieval king was called "father of the people" not as a metaphor, but as a moral reality. Just as a father exists to serve the good of his household rather than himself, so the king existed to serve the common good rather than his own will. When politics is ordered toward man's true end, paternal authority is not tyranny, but care.[234]

---

[233] **Ernst Kantorowicz**, *The King's Two Bodies* (1957), drawing on medieval coronation theology and dynastic responsibility.

[234] **St. Robert Bellarmine**, *De Laicis*, Book III (on political authority as ministerial and ordered to the common good).

Chapter 7: The Republic, A Bureaucratic Oligarchy by Another Name

Christendom's paternal understanding of kingship also explains why medieval political authority was personal rather than ideological. A father cannot rule anonymously, and neither could a king. His face, his lineage, and his reputation mattered. His failures were remembered. His virtues were imitated. Authority was embodied, not abstract. In contrast, modern systems dissolve responsibility into offices, procedures, and bureaucracies, where no one truly fathers the nation and no one is personally accountable for its moral direction.[235]

The king ruled as a known man, not an anonymous office. Loyalty was tied to personhood and national identity, not ideology.[236] The issue of the republic

---

[235] **Alexis de Tocqueville**, *The Old Regime and the Revolution*, Book I (on the loss of personal authority and rise of bureaucratic abstraction).

[236] **Marc Bloch**, *The Royal Touch* (1924), esp. Book I, on the personal and symbolic nature of medieval kingship

and the democracy is not merely that they are ineffective, but that they replace persons with systems.[237] For fear of the rise of a dictator, modern man has dispersed power across committees, departments and agencies.[238] Instead of one man who can be held personally responsible for outcomes, blamed for failures, and brought to justice, we now face a mass of interchangeable actors, nearly all motivated by self-interest.[239] Failure can always be blamed on "the system," never on a ruler. Yet rather than correcting the system, society calls for revolution once again, often at the urging of a vocal minority.[240]

It is commonly believed that a system without a single central ruler can be more directly governed by those at the bottom. This idea, the so-called "will of the people," is a political fiction.[241] Millions of

---

and loyalty rooted in the king's person rather than abstract institutions.

237 **Aristotle**, *Politics*, Book III, ch. 6–7, where regimes are defined by who rules and for what end, not by impersonal procedures.

238 **Alexis de Tocqueville**, *Democracy in America*, Vol. II, Part IV, ch. 6, describing the diffusion of power into administrative bodies and soft despotism.

239 **Max Weber**, *Economy and Society*, Vol. I, ch. 3, on bureaucratic authority as rule by offices rather than persons.

240 **Polybius**, *Histories*, Book VI, on anacyclosis and the recurring cycle of regime decay and popular revolt.

241 **Jean-Jacques Rousseau**, *The Social Contract*, Book II, ch. 3, defining the "general will" as distinct from the

individuals with conflicting desires cannot possess a single will.[242] Instead of participating directly through local institutions such as guilds, parishes, or estates, modern citizens cast a ballot every few years and pretend it constitutes real agency.[243] It rarely does, because once elected, rulers act independently of voters.[244] The vote, in the democratic sense, is a substitute for lived participation.[245] Tyranny under this system is no less real than under a single dictator, and is arguably worse precisely because it is less visible.[246]

If voting is not a true means of governance, then what function does it actually serve? In practice,

---

sum of individual wills, implicitly acknowledging its fragility.

[242] **James Madison**, *Federalist No. 10*, admitting the impossibility of a unified popular will due to faction and conflicting interests.

[243] **Edmund Burke**, *Speech to the Electors of Bristol* (1774), rejecting the notion that representation is mere obedience to voters' momentary wishes.

[244] **Thomas Hobbes**, *Leviathan*, ch. 16–18, on the independence of sovereign authority once consent has been given.

[245] **G. K. Chesterton**, *What's Wrong with the World* (1910), esp. Part I, critiquing voting as a thin substitute for real social participation.

[246] **Alexis de Tocqueville**, *Democracy in America*, Vol. II, Part IV, ch. 7, on democratic despotism being more pervasive precisely because it is less visible and less personal.

elections do not restrain power, but distort it.[247] They replace long-term responsibility with short-term popularity, and governance with perpetual campaigning.[248] This system presents itself as one in which rotating leaders allow intelligence and merit to rise, rather than leaving the fate of the nation to hereditary succession, as monarchy supposedly does. Yet in reality, only those with wealth, institutional backing, and media access can realistically win elections.[249]

Kings did not need to persuade the public of their legitimate authority.[250] Their task was to rule well, not to win favor.[251] When authority is maintained

---

[247] **Aristotle**, *Politics*, Book IV, ch. 4–6, where democracy is described as a regime prone to demagoguery and distortion of the common good through popular mechanisms.
[248] **Alexis de Tocqueville**, *Democracy in America*, Vol. II, Part I, ch. 2 and Part IV, ch. 6, on short-term political incentives and permanent agitation under democratic systems.
[249] **Federal Election Commission (FEC)**, *Campaign Finance Data* (U.S. House and Senate, 1980–present); see also **Center for Responsive Politics (OpenSecrets)**, documenting that candidates who outspend opponents win over 85–90% of the time in federal elections.
[250] **Marc Bloch**, *The Royal Touch*, Book I, on hereditary legitimacy as pre-political and not dependent on persuasion or consent.
[251] **Saint Thomas Aquinas**, *De Regno*, Book I, ch. 1–3, where the ruler's task is defined as ordering society

primarily through short-term popularity rather than long-term obligation, policy becomes reactive, incoherent, and unstable.[252] Rivalries emerge in the form of political parties, as each side struggles to retain power, sowing bitterness and resentment rather than unity.[253] This instability is not accidental. It flows directly from the philosophy that underlies modern political thought.

---

toward the common good rather than securing popular approval.

[252] **Max Weber**, *Politics as a Vocation* (1919), on politics under mass democracy becoming reactive, opportunistic, and oriented toward retention of power rather than principled rule.

[253] **James Madison**, *Federalist No. 10* and **George Washington**, *Farewell Address* (1796), both warning that factionalism is an inherent and corrosive feature of party-based systems.

Chapter 8: The Cult of Equality

Whenever democracy is critiqued, Americans tend to respond by insisting that the United States is a "republic, not a democracy."[254] This statement is similar to the claim that "ice is not liquid." True enough, yet both are composed of the same substance. Water remains water whether frozen or fluid, and rule by popular sovereignty remains rule by popular sovereignty whether it expresses itself directly or through representatives.[255] A republic may slow the process, filter it, or soften its effects, but it does not alter the underlying principle that authority originates from the collective will rather than from an objective moral order above it.[256]

---

[254] Federalist No. 39, **James Madison**, discussing the republican form of government and its foundations; see Avalon Project, Yale Law School, "The Federalist No. 39."

[255] **James Madison**, "The Federalist No. 10," on the practical distinction between a democracy and a republic and the delegation of government to representatives. Avalon Project, Yale Law School, "The Federalist No. 10."

[256] **Jean-Jacques Rousseau**, *The Social Contract* (1762), on sovereignty and the general will as the source of legitimate authority. See Book I–II

The distinction between democracy and republicanism is therefore one of form rather than substance. In a pure democracy, the people rule immediately. In a republic, they rule through elected officials, institutions, and procedures. Yet in both systems, legitimacy is ultimately grounded not in truth, virtue, or divine law, but in consent.[257] Power flows upward from numbers, not downward from responsibility. The vote remains the final justification for authority, even if it is delayed, diluted, or refined through constitutional mechanisms.

This matters because a system cannot rise above the philosophy that animates it. Whether democratic or republican, a regime founded on popular will must eventually treat all wills as equal, all opinions as interchangeable, and all authority as provisional. From this premise flows the modern obsession with equality not as shared dignity, but as sameness of function and voice. Once this assumption is accepted, hierarchy becomes suspect, moral judgment becomes coercion, and wisdom is replaced by ubiquity.[258]

---

[257] Tocqueville on equality and leveling tendencies in democratic societies and their social consequences; see *Democracy in America*, "Tyranny of the Majority."

[258] Tocqueville on equality and leveling tendencies in democratic societies and their social consequences; see *Democracy in America*, "Tyranny of the Majority."

Democracy and republicanism may differ slightly in structure, yet they share a common anthropology. Both assume that political authority is best generated by aggregating preferences rather than discerning truth. Both flatten qualitative distinctions into quantitative measures. Both inevitably drift toward centralization, moral relativism, and ideological rule, even as they promise freedom and participation.[259]

I refer to this idea of popular sovereignty as a "cult" because its foundations are, in a very real sense, religious. As stated earlier, religion will always inform politics, because politics is simply applied belief about man and his purpose. While feudal monarchy was informed by the Cult of the Saints, popular sovereignty is informed by the Cult of Equality. If one tells the average modern American, for example, that ordinary people ought not possess an inherent right to vote, he recoils in fear of totalitarian rule. The reflexive response is almost always the same: "All people should have a say." Yet this reaction rarely proceeds from careful reasoning. More often, it arises from emotional conditioning and moral instinct shaped by modern dogma. The vote is treated not as a practical tool of

---

[259] Madison and Tocqueville on aggregation of preferences and institutional drift; see Federalist No. 10 and Tocqueville, *Democracy in America*. [Federalist No. 10]

governance, but as a sacred rite, the visible sign of one's dignity and worth. To question it is not perceived as a political disagreement, but as a kind of heresy. In this way, democracy functions less as a system of rule and more as a faith, complete with unquestioned axioms, moral taboos, and articles of belief that must be affirmed regardless of their consequences.[260]

If authority derives only from the people, then truth becomes functionally undecidable. Long before modern democracy, people in the West had already begun subscribing to the "Enlightenment" notion that truth could never be fully known.[261] It followed naturally that a political system informed by this philosophy would be embraced. The consequences of such a worldview are the erasure of local distinctions and the relocation of decision making to distant, supposedly "neutral" authorities. The logical conclusion of this ideology is now visible everywhere: chaos, disorder, and misery. Yet this disorder has roots. Under Catholic monarchy,

---

[260] **Robert N. Bellah**, "Civil Religion in America," *Daedalus* 96, no. 1 (Winter 1967), on the quasi-religious role of civic rites and beliefs; and scholarly discussion of "civil religion" as a form of public faith.

[261] David Hume's view that matters of fact cannot be justified with certainty is described in *Britannica's* article on 18th-century skepticism, noting that Hume found causal reasoning and knowledge of the external world epistemologically dubious.

authority was distributed according to competence and proximity. Now it is flattened into abstraction.[262]

By substituting wisdom, inheritance, and responsibility with numerical majorities, authority is justified by procedure rather than virtue. Popular sovereignty does not merely change who rules; it rests on the claim that human dignity requires sameness: sameness of role, sameness of voice, and sameness of status. This is egalitarianism. It does not affirm equality before God, but equality in *every sense.* It is a denial of meaningful hierarchy, distinction, and ordered authority, all in the name of "liberation." Medieval philosophy is therefore painted as archaic by modern thinkers, precisely because it presupposes inequality of role rather than inequality of dignity. To the liberal ideologue, however, inequality of any kind is treated as inequality of worth.

---

[262] **John Locke**, *Essay Concerning Human Understanding* (1690), and the rise of modern empiricism and epistemic limits that influenced Enlightenment political thought; see Book IV on knowledge and its limits.

Chapter 9: Right Wing Versus Left Wing: A False Binary

Legacy media and far left ideologues routinely lament what they call the "radicalization" of young men.[263] From renewed religious devotion[264] to the expression of sympathy for historical figures like Joseph Stalin and Adolf Hitler,[265] men of Generation Z now hold views that would have been unthinkable to much of the late twentieth century,

---

[263] Pew Research Center reports on how media and political commentators express concern about online radicalization among young people: "Many Americans See News Media 'Too Liberal,'" *Pew Research Center*, 26 May 2020

[264] **Pew Research Center**. *Religious Landscape Study*, Feb. 26, 2025

[265] "White Nationalist Nick Fuentes Calls Hitler 'F***ing Cool' during Piers Morgan Interview." *Yahoo News UK.*, Leingang, Rachel. "Tucker Carlson's Interview with Far-Right Antisemite Nick Fuentes Divides Conservatives." *The Guardian*, 31 Oct. 2025 and Nick Fuentes has publicly stated that he admires certain aspects of figures such as Joseph Stalin and Adolf Hitler while disclaiming endorsement of their crimes, framing his remarks as an attempt to demystify figures he believes are treated as ultimate evils rather than subjects of historical analysis.

and even to mainstream culture only a few years ago. Both the elderly and the ideological extremes, those nearing the end of their influence and those long divorced from reality, react with alarm to the "shocking" behavior of young men for whom they have often expressed open contempt for decades.[266]

The irony of this narrative is that these young men are not especially radical by historical standards. This is not to say that all their conclusions are correct, but rather that many of their instincts and assumptions have been commonly held by men across civilizations for centuries. What is genuinely radical is not their return to older ways of thinking, but the ideological distance traveled by modern liberalism itself. Many liberals, particularly among the baby boomer generation and their cultural heirs, have moved so far from the historical norm that

---

[266] **Christina Hoff Sommers**, *The War Against Boys*: This book directly argues that modern education systems and media narratives portray masculinity as pathological and boys as defective. It explicitly addresses cultural hostility toward men and boys. **See also Paul Nathanson and Katherine K. Young,** *Legalizing Misandry*: This is one of the clearest academic arguments that Western institutions, including media, normalize contempt for men under the guise of equality discourse. **See also Warren Farrell and John Gray**, *The Boy Crisis*: This work documents how media, education, and cultural narratives disproportionately blame or marginalize men and boys, especially working-class and fatherless males.

they are no longer merely mistaken, but profoundly disconnected from reality.

This disconnection became unmistakable for many when segments of the liberal public openly mocked and celebrated the assassination of Charlie Kirk, an act that should have been universally condemned as a moral evil regardless of political disagreement. The same voices that had previously rioted over the death of a criminal who died of a fentanyl overdose[267] while resisting arrest expressed moral outrage once again over the death of Renee Good. This was despite the obvious fact that her actions directly precipitated the use of lethal force.[268] To

---

[267] Hennepin County Medical Examiner's Office. *Autopsy Report: George Floyd, ME No. 20-3700.* DocumentCloud: This autopsy reveals that Floyd, thought to have been murdered by police, actually suffered no life threatening injuries. He was revealed to, however, have a fatal amount of fentanyl in his system, at 11 ng/ml. Despite this fact, all four police officers who detained him were convicted of murder, despite the fact that their actions could not have caused his death. **See** Chauvin's sentences and prison transfer: *WUSF* and AP coverage, Chauvin's 22½-year state sentence and 21-year federal sentence, plus stabbing details: *Police1*, Lane's sentences and release: *WUSF*, Kueng's sentence details and prison location/release: *WUSF* and Corrections1 summary and Thao's sentence details and prison location/release: *WUSF* and Corrections1 summary. This is one of many examples of how widespread liberal ideology leads to grave injustice.

[268] See *"Minneapolis ICE Shooting: New Video From DHS Shows What Led Up to Shooting." FOX 9*

those with a functioning conscience, including many who hold otherwise liberal views,[269] such reactions are not only absurd, but deeply disturbing.

Yet once one understands that the logical conclusion of modern liberalism is the denial of objective truth in favor of subjective reality, these reactions become intelligible. When truth is no longer something to which one submits, but something one constructs, moral judgment collapses into emotional alignment. Violence is condemned or excused not based on justice, but on ideological loyalty. What

---

Minneapolis-St. Paul and *"Officer's Cellphone Video Captures Moments Leading Up to Fatal ICE Shooting." ABC15 Scripps News*, which show both Good and her partner provoking ICE agents after impeding law enforcement, and Good nearly running over an officer in front of her car. **See also Gooding, Dan, and Gabe Whisnant.** "ICE Agent Suffered Internal Bleeding After Minneapolis Shooting." *Newsweek*, 14 Jan. 2026, which reports that officer who shot her suffered internal bleeding. If hadn't shot her, he would not have lived. If she had complied with the officers, or better yet, never been there in the first place, she would still be alive.

[269] *"The Woke Wave and Left Liberalism."* The Narrative World, 3 Sept. 2024, A blog post discusses that one YouTuber named **Amir Odom** said he left the left and criticized "woke ideology" and aspects of contemporary left-liberal culture, including identity politics and pop culture changes he saw as excessive. **See also Williams, Thomas Chatterton.** *Summer of Our Discontent: The Age of Certainty and the Demise of Discourse*. 2025.

appears insane is, in fact, the consistent outworking of a worldview untethered from reality itself.

Aquinas, Ripperger, Amorth: Liberalism and Demonic Psychology

According to Aquinas, truth is *adaequatio intellectus et rei*, or the conformity of the intellect to reality.[270] When the will dominates the intellect, truth is no longer received but imposed. Aquinas teaches that sin disorders the faculties, causing the will to command the intellect to justify desire rather than submit to truth.[271] Liberalism does precisely this. It elevates desire, identity, and emotion above objective reality. Moral judgments become expressions of preference rather than conclusions drawn from reason. This is why contradictory positions can be held simultaneously without discomfort. The intellect is no longer ordered toward truth, but conscripted to defend the will.

Renowned exorcist Fr. Chad Ripperger observes from his experience that demonic influence does not usually begin with overt evil, but with the

---

[270] Thomas Aquinas defines truth as the conformity of intellect and reality: **Aquinas, Thomas**. *Summa Theologiae*. Part I, Q. 16, Art. 1.

[271] On sin's effect on the intellect and will: **Aquinas, Thomas**. *Summa Theologiae*. Part I–II, Q. 79, Arts. 1–4.

systematic inversion of reality.[272] Demons distort perception, exaggerate grievance, and collapse moral categories. One of their primary tactics is emotional reasoning: *"I feel, therefore it is true."*[273]

This maps directly onto modern ideological behavior. Violence is condemned or praised depending on who commits it. Victimhood is assigned based on identity, not action. Responsibility is erased when it conflicts with narrative. These are not random errors, but consistent patterns of disordered cognition.

Fr. Gabriele Amorth, an influential exorcist for the Diocese of Rome, emphasized that demons hate hierarchy, order, and objective authority because these reflect God Himself.[274] Amorth's writings on the nature of evil describe how secular and spiritual

---

[272] Chad Ripperger discusses demonology and perception in his recorded talks available through the Aquinas Institute: **Ripperger, Chad**. *Demonology Audio Lectures*, AquinasInstitute.org

[273] Ripperger's description of demonic strategy ("I feel, therefore it is true") is paraphrased from his teachings on emotional reasoning as a tactic of spiritual deception; see **ibid**.

[274] **Amorth, Gabriele**. *An Exorcist Explains the Demonic: The Antics of Satan and His Army of Fallen Angels.* Sophia Institute Press, 2016. (This is the primary published book where Amorth discusses *how demons act against divine order, authority, and obedience*; see book description and contents that frame his theology of demonic action.)

disorder attacks reason, obedience, and submission to God, akin to how demons disrupt order and authority.[275] They prefer chaos, contradiction, and resentment. A society that rejects fatherhood, hierarchy, and moral absolutes, as our liberal society does, mirrors this hatred of order almost perfectly.[276] This may explain the political left's indiscriminate hatred for law enforcement. Any and all use of force by the state, according to these liberals, is "totalitarian." Demons believe much the same about created order itself. This may help explain the political left's indiscriminate hostility toward law enforcement. Any use of force by the state, according to these liberals, is reflexively labeled "totalitarian." Demons, notably, hold a similar contempt for created order itself. This outrage, however, is conspicuously absent when the state engages in genuinely totalitarian behavior,

---

[275] **Amorth, Gabriele**. "The second is the release from the principle of authority, that is, from any obligation to obey parents, the Church, the state, and whoever places restrictions in the name of the common good." Idib (This quote directly supports the idea that demonic influence opposes authority and divine order.)

[276] **Amorth, Gabriele**. In accounts of his exorcism ministry, demons are quoted as **hating holy authority and the Mass**, which reinforces the claim that demonic opposition is against hierarchy and objective authority: "The Mass is our torment; every Eucharist burns us." "The Pope [John Paul II] hurts us with his prayers."
— From recorded demon confessions during exorcisms reported by Amorth.

such as the COVID-era restrictions[277] or Zohran Mamdani's shameless proposal to tax white citizens and redistribute their wealth on explicitly racial grounds.[278] Extreme leftist ideologues, in these circumstances, suddenly find no objection to force when it is used to humiliate, punish, or make ordinary people miserable.

At the same time, the modern right and left have developed two opposing and parallel moral systems.[279] Each side operates according to a different set of sacred taboos and permissible transgressions.[280] To the left, jokes blaspheming Our Lord are trivial or even virtuous, while jokes about women or non-white racial groups are treated as horrific and unthinkable crimes.[281] To the right-wing

---

[277] **Bickerton, James**. "Zohran Mamdani Proposes Taxing 'Whiter Neighborhoods' in NYC." Newsweek, 27 June 2025

[278] **Baumann, Beth**. "Grocery Store Manager's Response to Maskless Women: Lock Them Inside Until Police Arrive." Townhall, 16 Aug. 2020

[279] **Pew Research Center**, *"Beyond Red vs. Blue: Political Typology"* and subsequent polarization studies (2014–2023), documenting moral, cultural, and worldview divergence between ideological groups.

[280] **Jonathan Haidt**, *The Righteous Mind* (2012); supplemented by Pew data on moral foundations and partisan moral priorities (statistical survey research).

[281] **Pew Research Center**, *"Views on Offensive Speech and Blasphemy"* (2017–2022), showing asymmetrical tolerance for religious offense versus protected-class offense.

Christian, the moral valuation is often reversed.[282] Adolf Hitler, to the right, is one brutal dictator among many in history; to the left, he is treated as Satan incarnate, the embodiment of absolute evil.[283] To the left, homosexuality is framed as normal and healthy; to the right, it is seen as an obvious distortion of nature.[284]

We have reached a point at which these parallel moral codes are so radically divergent that reasonable discourse has become nearly impossible.[285] This breakdown is made worse when the left increasingly finds it acceptable to issue death threats against ideological opponents, rationalizing such behavior as "righteous anger" or "resistance."[286] A small number on the right, though

---

[282] **Pew Research Center**, *"Religious Landscape Study"* (2014; updates 2019–2023), documenting moral issue divergence between practicing Christians and secular liberals.

[283] YouGov polling on historical villains and moral salience (2018–2022), showing disproportionate symbolic focus on Hitler among left-leaning respondents compared to other mass killers.

[284] **Gallup**, *"Moral Acceptability of Homosexuality"* (1987–2023), showing stark ideological splits on the issue.

[285] **Pew Research Center**, *"Political Polarization in the American Public"* (2014; updated 2020, 2023), documenting the collapse of cross-ideological discourse and rising social hostility.

[286] U.S. Department of Justice & FBI statistics on threats against public officials and private citizens (2016–2023),

far fewer, have mirrored this behavior in retaliation.[287] The answer to this collapse is not nihilistic violence or mutual bitterness, but a return to law, justice, order, and objective truth.

When ideology rejects authority, denies natural distinctions, and dissolves responsibility into emotion, it produces the very psychological conditions that Father Amorth repeatedly identified in cases of obsession and possession: confusion, rage, moral inversion, and a perverse delight in destruction cloaked as justice.[288] Liberalism does not merely err politically. It disorders the intellect, inverts moral judgment, and habituates the soul to unreality. In this sense, its psychological fruits bear a striking resemblance to what the Church has long

---

including ideological motivation breakdowns; see also DHS threat assessments.

[287] FBI Domestic Terrorism Reports (2020–2023), noting retaliatory threats and violence across ideological lines, with asymmetry in frequency depending on year and context.

[288] **Amorth, Gabriele**. *An Exorcist Explains the Demonic: The Antics of Satan and His Army of Fallen Angels*. Sophia Institute Press, 2016., In his account of demonic activity and spiritual disorder, Amorth consistently presents *the Devil and fallen angels as forces that disrupt reason, obedience to legitimate authority, and moral order* by attacking human tendencies toward sin and confusion. This foundational book outlines how spiritual evil leads to disordered thought, temptations, and moral upheaval, which parallels your description of ideological rejection of authority and collapse of moral judgment.

recognized as demonic patterns of thought. For this reason, Archbishop Marcel Lefebvre famously described liberalism as a "disease of the mind."[289]

Of course, this condition did not arise overnight. Politics had been moving in this direction for centuries, beginning, I would argue, with the Protestant Revolution. That rupture was not merely theological, but philosophical and psychological. It marked the first large-scale rejection of ecclesial authority in favor of private judgment. Once the authority of the Church was denied, the authority of the monarchy soon followed. After the monarchy fell, the nobility was dismantled. When aristocratic order collapsed, the capitalist class was targeted. Finally, with feminism, even the natural authority of the father within the family was rejected. What appears as a series of disconnected political revolutions is in fact a single ideological domino effect: the systematic destruction of hierarchy itself.

At its core lies a fundamental distinction that modern discourse obscures. What is commonly labeled "right" is not merely a political position, but a disposition that recognizes hierarchy, nature, order, and tradition as real and binding. What is

---

[289] Archbishop Marcel Lefebvre's critique of modernism and liberal influence is documented in SSPX sources, e.g., "**The Spirit of Liberalism Has Penetrated the Church**," in *Apologia pro Marcel Lefebvre* (1980)

labeled “left” is not simply a preference for reform, but an ideological impulse to remake man, society, and morality according to abstract theory. One begins with reality and submits to it; the other begins with an idea and forces reality to conform.

This is why monarchy cannot properly be called “right-wing” in the modern sense. It is pre-ideological. It does not arise from theory, but from the natural structure of authority, inheritance, obligation, and responsibility. Modern politics, by contrast, reduces man to an interchangeable unit: an economic actor, a voter, a demographic category. Traditional monarchy elevated man by situating him within a meaningful hierarchy ordered toward the common good, where authority was personal and responsibility unavoidable.

The purpose of this chapter, then, is not to defend one modern faction against another, but to demonstrate that modern “right–left” divide is a false binary. What are called conservatives, along with many less extreme liberals, are in reality liberals who have not followed their own premises to their logical conclusion. That conclusion is too unsettling to accept. Instead, they cling to earlier, milder forms of liberalism out of attachment to lesser goods: comfort, stability, familiarity, while remaining unwilling or unable to confront the deeper truth.

These are not necessarily bad people. But they are, intellectually speaking, stagnant. The ideological train continues to move because its logic demands motion. Leftist ideologues continue to drive it forward, while moderates and conservatives have jumped off at earlier stations after glimpsing the destination. They remain puzzled, however, as to why the train does not stop, unwilling to admit that the problem is not the speed, but the track itself.

Part 4: Freedom Under Monarchy, Tyranny Under Democracy - A Historical Paradox

Chapter 10: Local Liberties in the Age of Kings

As discussed earlier, the lower classes in medieval society enjoyed many real and tangible freedoms, much to the chagrin of modern man. It is often objected that whatever liberties medieval people possessed, they lacked one freedom now considered indispensable: religious freedom. To this objection, I ask a simple question: so what? What medieval society lacked in the abstract freedom to choose between religions was more than compensated for by the possession of concrete, lived freedoms that modern people no longer enjoy.

This objection rests on a failure to define freedom properly. Archbishop Marcel Lefebvre addresses this confusion directly in *They Have Uncrowned Him*, where he distinguishes between false freedom and true freedom.[290] False freedom is the ability to choose anything whatsoever, including error, vice, and self-destruction. True freedom, by contrast, is

---

[290] **Marcel Lefebvre**, *They Have Uncrowned Him*, Angelus Press, ch. 2–3.

the freedom to pursue the good without obstruction.[291] It is not freedom *from* truth, but freedom *for* truth. A man is not made free by being offered poison alongside bread, but by being protected from poison altogether.[292]

Medieval Christendom understood freedom in this older and more realistic sense. Men were free to live rightly within a moral order that was assumed to be true.[293] They were free to raise families, practice trades, worship God, govern their communities, and inherit a way of life without constant interference.[294] The absence of religious pluralism did not produce tyranny; it produced coherence.[295] Modern man, offered infinite choices yet deprived of stability, confuses abundance of options with freedom.[296]

Once freedom is understood not as limitless choice but as protected participation in a just and ordered society, the political structure of the Middle Ages

---

[291] **Ibid**.; see also St. Thomas Aquinas, *Summa Theologiae*, I–II, q. 90, a. 1 (law ordered to the good).
[292] Lefebvre, *They Have Uncrowned Him*, discussion of liberty versus license.
[293] **St. Thomas Aquinas**, *Summa Contra Gentiles*, Book III, ch. 128–130.
[294] Medieval town charters and guild statutes; see *The Charter of Lorris* (c. 1155).
[295] **Pope Leo XIII**, *Libertas Praestantissimum* (1888), §§14–18.
[296] **Alexis de Tocqueville**, *Democracy in America*, Vol. II, Part II, ch. 6.

begins to make sense.[297] Liberty did not exist in the abstract, nor was it dispensed from above by ideology. It was exercised locally, concretely, and communally.[298] This brings us directly to the real mechanisms by which ordinary people governed their own lives: the self-governing towns, charters, and customary rights of commoners.[299]

During the tenth through fourteenth centuries, European societies under feudal monarchy saw the steady growth of towns and cities.[300] These towns were populated by various professionals, the "townsmen" first introduced in Chapter Two.[301] Townsmen did not acquire their rights through slogans, abstract declarations, or revolutions, but through charters.[302] Charters were binding legal contracts between a town community and a king or lord.[303] They enumerated specific rights that were enforceable in court and could be appealed to higher

---

[297] **Aquinas**, *De Regno*, Book I, ch. 1–2.
[298] **Johannes Althusius**, *Politica* (1603), ch. I–III (preserving medieval subsidiarity).
[299] Magna Carta (1215); various municipal charters of Paris, Florence, and Cologne.
[300] **Henri Pirenne**, *Medieval Cities: Their Origins and the Revival of Trade*
[301] **Jacques Le Goff**, *Medieval Civilization*
[302] **Susan Reynolds**, *Kingdoms and Communities in Western Europe, 900–1300*
[303] **Marc Bloch**, *Feudal Society*, Vol. I

authorities, including the crown and the Church.[304] These rights were concrete, local, inherited, and limited to particular communities.[305] They included the right to self-taxation, to hold courts, to regulate markets, and even to elect local officials.[306] In this way, political participation was exercised not through distant representation, but through direct, daily governance at the level where life was actually lived.[307]

Through self-taxation, towns could collect their own revenues and decide collectively how those funds were used.[308] Whatever taxes the king received were typically fixed annual payments rather than arbitrary or constantly expanding levies.[309] This arrangement protected towns from sudden confiscation of property and from the endless new taxes that modern people are routinely subjected to.[310] Towns elected mayors, aldermen, and councils, many of whom were members of local guilds and lived among the people they governed.[311]

---

[304] **Bracton**, *De Legibus et Consuetudinibus Angliae*, c. 1235
[305] **Philippe de Beaumanoir**, *Coutumes de Beauvaisis*
[306] *Charter of Lorris* (text preserved in French municipal archives)
[307] **Otto of Freising**, *Gesta Friderici Imperatoris*
[308] *Statutes of the City of London*, 12th–13th c.
[309] Magna Carta, 1215, clauses 12, 14
[310] **Eileen Power**, *Medieval People*
[311] *Liber Albus* (London), 1419

These elections were limited, practical, and based on reputation and service rather than party ideology.[312] Towns also regulated their own markets, setting prices for essential goods, controlling weights and measures, and inspecting products for quality.[313] Such measures prevented price gouging, fraud, and exploitation by outside merchants.[314]

A key example of this system is the well-known Magna Carta. It is often taught in modern classrooms as a "democratic" document. In reality, it was drafted to protect the rights of towns and nobles alike.[315] It guaranteed ancient liberties, due process, and clear limits on arbitrary taxation.[316] The lesser-known Charter of Lorris became a model charter throughout France during the eleventh and twelfth centuries.[317] It granted towns fixed rents, legal protections, and freedom from arbitrary interference by lords.[318] These provisions

---

312 *Statuta Communis Florentiae*, 13th c.
313 *Assize of Bread and Ale* (England, 13th c.)
314 **Jean Gimpel**, *The Medieval Machine*
315 **J.C. Holt**, *Magna Carta*
316 Magna Carta, clauses 39–41
317 *Charte de Lorris*, c. 1155
318 **Georges Duby**, *Rural Economy and Country Life in the Medieval West*

encouraged economic stability and sustained urban growth.[319]

Charters were public, written, and sworn under oath.[320] For any official to violate a charter was both difficult and dangerous, as it risked revolt, excommunication, and the loss of legitimacy.[321] Kings were therefore incentivized to defend towns against corrupt nobles, since towns provided stable revenue and social order.[322] Nobles, in turn, were restrained by charters from making arbitrary arrests, increasing rents without grave cause, or manipulating local markets.[323] Rights under this system were not abstract claims, but lived practices.[324] Medieval liberty was not theoretical, nor did it need to be sustained by constant violence or ideological movements.[325] It was communal, stable, protected by authority, and passed from parent to child.[326] It was attached to inheritance rather than ideology.[327] Commoners were not

---

319 **Henri Pirenne**, *Economic and Social History of Medieval Europe*
320 Medieval charter formulae, *Monumenta Germaniae Historica*
321 **Gregory IX**, *Liber Extra* (on oaths and contracts)
322 **Orderic Vitalis**, *Ecclesiastical History*
323 *Sachsenspiegel*, early 13th c.
324 **Marc Bloch**, *Feudal Society*
325 **Dom Prosper Guéranger**, *The Liturgical Year* (social order reflections)
326 **Philippe Ariès**, *Centuries of Childhood*
327 **Régine Pernoud**, *Those Terrible Middle Ages!*

governed by distant authorities, but by one another, where life actually took place.[328] The duty of higher authorities, the crown and the Church, was to protect these local rights.[329] For this reason, medieval peasants and townsmen often exercised more real control over the conditions of their daily lives than modern citizens who participate only through distant and symbolic political gestures.[330]

Serfs, who most often lived in rural areas, possessed far more rights and freedoms than modern people tend to realize.[331] The relationship between serfs and their lords was not unilateral, but reciprocal.[332] Rather than resembling that of a slave and a master, it more closely resembled a modern relationship between tenant and landlord.[333] Unlike a modern landlord, however, a medieval lord was legally obligated to provide military protection, aid during

---

[328] **Christopher Brooke**, *The Twelfth-Century Renaissance*
[329] Council records preserved in *Liberius.net*
[330] **Alexis de Tocqueville**, *Democracy in America* (comparative observation)
[331] **Polyptych of Irminon** (c. 823), detailed records of peasant rights, obligations, and protections on Carolingian estates.
[332] **Marc Bloch**, *Les caractères originaux de l'histoire rurale française* (drawing directly from medieval manorial records).
[333] **Leges Henrici Primi** (early 12th c.), chs. 70–75, distinctions between servitude and slavery under English law.

famine or disaster, and the defense of his serfs' customary rights.[334]

Abusive lords did not act with impunity. They faced the real possibility of peasant revolt, correction by the king, intervention by higher nobles, and punishment by the Church.[335] Disputes between serfs and lords were handled in various local courts, depending on the severity of the offense.[336] Serfs were bound to the land, but not imprisoned by it. They could purchase their freedom through manumission, relocate with permission, or improve their status over time.[337]

Serfdom existed not to enslave the lower classes, but to guarantee access to land, housing, and food, to prevent mass displacement, and to anchor families within stable communities.[338] Before the Black Death weakened the institution, it functioned as a system that provided even the less capable or less ambitious with a means of subsistence and a

---

[334] **Capitularies of Charlemagne**, esp. *Capitulare de Villis*, obligations of lords toward dependents.
[335] **Fourth Lateran Council (1215)**, ecclesiastical penalties for unjust rulers; grounds for excommunication.
[336] **Manorial Court Rolls** (England, 13th–14th c.), surviving records of serfs suing lords and vice versa.
[337] **Bracton**, *De Legibus et Consuetudinibus Angliae*, manumission, villein status, and legal remedies.
[338] **Customals** (e.g., *Custumal of Beauvaisis* by Philippe de Beaumanoir, c. 1283).

recognized place in society.[339] To the surprise of many, the medieval serf often enjoyed more real security and practical autonomy than the average modern salary worker.[340] Medieval serfs lacked abstract freedoms, but possessed concrete stability. Modern workers possess abstract rights, yet often lack both security and rootedness.

---

[339] **Jean Froissart**, *Chronicles*, social effects of the Black Death on labor obligations.

[340] **Statute of Labourers (1351)**, evidence that pre-plague serfs had enough leverage that wages had to be forcibly suppressed afterward.

Chapter 11: The Modern State: Centralized, Surveillance-Driven, and Impersonal

When the limited yet concrete rights of peasants and serfs are compared to those of the modern wage worker, the contrast is striking. A modern man must not only obtain, but continually maintain, his most basic necessities, shelter, water, food, and, in the modern era, electricity, by constant wage labor.[341] Bishop Richard Williamson observed in a lecture given in 1999 that the modern man believes himself to be "free," even though he must endlessly work for wages in order to pay for a home he does not truly own. If he cannot pay, he may be evicted and rendered homeless, regardless of circumstance.[342]

---

[341] **Karl Polanyi**, *The Great Transformation* (1944), chs. 6–7.
[342] **Matthew Desmond**, *Evicted: Poverty and Profit in the American City* (2016).

Williamson rightly noted that this is not freedom, but a form of economic servitude.[343]

Shelter is a basic human need, yet under modern capitalism it is treated as a speculative commodity, a financial instrument to be gambled on, or an "investment" rather than a home.[344] When homelessness explodes and home ownership becomes an impossible dream for ordinary people, both the naïve and the greedy express confusion when millions turn toward socialist policies in desperation.[345] Although the leaders of socialist movements may be malicious, their movements gain traction not from envy, but from instability created by a system that has severed basic human needs from security, place, and inheritance.[346]

Our present condition is the result of a deeper transformation in how society is governed: the

---

343 **Bishop Richard Williamson**, *Conference on Catholic Social Teaching and Modern Society*, 1999 (SSPX archive recordings).
344 **Thomas Piketty**, *Capital in the Twenty-First Century* (2014), Part II.
345 U.S. Department of Housing and Urban Development (HUD), *Annual Homeless Assessment Report*, latest available data.
346 **Friedrich Engels**, *The Condition of the Working Class in England* (1845), Preface.

replacement of local, personal authority with centralized, abstract administration.[347]

Medieval society understood order as something received, not designed. Authority flowed from God, through nature, through custom, and into concrete institutions such as the family, parish, guild, and lordship.[348] Law was not invented to achieve an ideal future, but articulated to preserve a lived order inherited from the past.[349] The “enlightenment" reversed this logic. Thinkers of this era increasingly claimed that society ought to be rebuilt from first principles, that tradition was a form of superstition, that custom was irrational unless justified by abstract reason, and that authority must be proven rather than inherited.[350] This shift undermined the rights of both the lower classes and the nobility, which depended upon inherited obligations, personal authority, and local variation.[351] According to so-called Enlightenment philosophy, feudal arrangements possessed no legitimate claim to existence precisely because they could not be

---

[347] **Max Weber**, *Economy and Society* (1922), on rational-legal authority.
[348] **St. Thomas Aquinas**, *Summa Theologiae*, I–II, q. 90–97.
[349] **Henry de Bracton**, *De Legibus et Consuetudinibus Angliae* (13th c.).
[350] **John Locke**, *Second Treatise of Government* (1689).
[351] **Marc Bloch**, *Feudal Society* (1939), Vol. I.

"proven" by reason alone.[352] By demanding that every right justify itself independently of history, custom, and lived practice, these thinkers did not secure freedom. They abolished it.

Under feudalism, rights existed because they were exercised. Liberties were presumed unless violated. Custom itself was proof of rights, and a man did not need to argue that he had a right; he *used it.*[353] Under the modern framework, a right existed only if it could be theoretically justified. Anything not defensible in abstract language was dismissed as arbitrary.[354] What had once been protected because it existed was now destroyed because it could not be explained. Customary rights did not vanish because they were unjust, but because they were local, inherited, and resistant to abstraction. What could not be systematized could not be tolerated.[355]

Once authority and rights were removed from custom, place, and personhood, they had to be relocated somewhere else. What could no longer be trusted to families, guilds, parishes, or local courts had to be administered from above.[356] The modern

---

352 **Jean-Jacques Rousseau**, *The Social Contract* (1762), Book I.
353 Magna Carta (1215), esp. clauses 39–41.
354 **Jeremy Bentham**, *Anarchical Fallacies* (1796).
355 **E.P. Thompson**, *Customs in Common* (1991).
356 **Alexis de Tocqueville**, *The Old Regime and the Revolution* (1856).

state emerged not merely as a governing body, but as a compensatory mechanism for the destruction of inherited order.[357] Because authority was no longer personal or customary, it became abstract, centralized, and procedural. Law ceased to be something known through lived experience and became something enforced through documentation, regulation, and constant oversight.[358]

A society built on theory rather than tradition cannot rely on trust; it must rely on verification. The more authority is detached from persons and places, the more it must observe, record, and manage from a distance.[359] The modern state did not merely centralize power. It required surveillance.[360] Citizens were no longer members of communities governed by shared obligation, but interchangeable units to be monitored, categorized, and regulated.[361] What had once been enforced by conscience, custom, and proximity now required bureaucracies, databases, permits, and compliance mechanisms. The modern administrative state is not an accident

---

[357] **James Scott**, *Seeing Like a State* (1998).
[358] **Michel Foucault**, *Discipline and Punish* (1975).
[359] **Max Weber**, *Bureaucracy*, in *From Max Weber: Essays in Sociology*.
[360] **Michel Foucault**, *Security, Territory, Population* (1977–78 lectures).
[361] **Hannah Arendt**, *The Origins of Totalitarianism* (1951).

of history; it is the logical outcome of a system that abandoned lived order in favor of abstract proof.

Chapter 12: True Freedom

Medieval Christians were not attached to religion and custom out of mere superstition. They upheld these things because they understood them to be necessary for the preservation of true freedom.[362] The principle is quite simple. A man may be free to bang randomly on the keys of a piano or to walk away from it altogether, but he is not free to *play* the piano until he has acquired the discipline and skill required to do so.[363] Modern philosophy, by contrast, would have us believe that the freedom to produce garbled noise is identical to the freedom to perform a sonata, and that the latter can only exist if the former is preserved without restraint. After all, one cannot "prove" that *Clair de Lune* is music while the smashing of piano keys is not.[364] The first is therefore reduced to mere preference, and the second elevated to the same status. Anything that cannot be proven by abstract reason is dismissed as subjective. The last century and a half have

---

362 **Augustine of Hippo**, *De Libero Arbitrio*, I.5–6
363 **Aristotle**, *Nicomachean Ethics*, II.1–4
364 **Plato**, *Republic*, Book X (on art, form, and meaning beyond mere perception), see also Immanuel Kant, *Critique of Judgment* (1790) for the opposing perspective.

demonstrated with brutal clarity that a society cannot be sustained by preference alone.[365]

Saint Thomas Aquinas teaches that freedom is not defined as the absence of constraint, but as the capacity to act in accordance with reason and the good.[366] Men were most free not when they could choose anything whatsoever, but when they were formed to choose well.[367] Virtue did not limit freedom; it made freedom possible. Just as the trained musician is freer than the novice, the virtuous man was understood to be freer than the unformed one. Law, custom, and authority were therefore not enemies of liberty, but its tutors.[368] They shaped the will toward what was true and good, enabling men to act deliberately rather than impulsively. Modern notions of freedom reverse this order, treating all formation as oppression and all restraint as tyranny. The result is not greater liberty, but moral incompetence: men technically

---

[365] **Alexis de Tocqueville**, *Democracy in America*, Vol. II, Part II, ch. 2–3
[366] **St. Thomas Aquinas**, *Summa Theologiae*, I–II, q. 90, a. 1; q. 91, a. 2
[367] **St. Thomas Aquinas**, *Summa Theologiae*, I–II, q. 17, a. 1
[368] **St. Thomas Aquinas**, *Summa Theologiae*, I–II, q. 95, a. 1

permitted to do everything, yet increasingly incapable of doing anything well.[369]

Authority, as Christendom understood it, was ordered toward moral formation, not mere control or efficiency. Kingship existed for the common good, not for abstract ideals of productivity, output, or ideological uniformity.[370] Law, under the guidance of the Church and the crown, functioned as a kind of moral grammar: a figurative guide for living well, much like a set of principles that teaches a man not merely to strike piano keys, but to play music.[371] In order to live rightly, the people had to know what was good, what was forbidden, and why both mattered. Feudal hierarchy, with its layered and reciprocal authorities restraining one another, provided the structure through which virtue could be learned and practiced.[372] Power was divided not to weaken society, but to protect it from

---

369 **Pope Leo XIII**, *Libertas Praestantissimum* (1888), §§7–9

370 **St. Thomas Aquinas**, *De Regno ad Regem Cypri*, I.1–2. Aquinas explicitly defines kingship as rule ordered to the *bonum commune* and contrasts it with tyranny, which seeks private benefit.

371 **St. Thomas Aquinas**, *Summa Theologiae*, I–II, q. 90, a. 1–2. Aquinas defines law as "an ordinance of reason for the common good," emphasizing its pedagogical and moral function.

372 **John of Salisbury**, *Policraticus*, Book IV. Salisbury describes society as an ordered body with distinct members whose mutual restraint preserves justice and harmony.

abuse, avarice, and the unchecked ambition that inevitably arises where authority is unaccountable.[373]

The foundation of society was, and has always been, the family. Just as kingship was understood as stewardship rather than domination, fatherhood within the household followed the same pattern.[374] The mother was recognized as the heart of the home, just as the queen was regarded as the heart of the kingdom, giving life, order, and continuity to what authority protected.[375] Father, mother, and children possessed unequal roles, yet equal dignity before God, and therefore equal worth before civilization itself.[376] Liberal philosophy, by contrast, increasingly treats the family as an obstacle to freedom rather than its source. Detached from inherited duty, natural hierarchy, and moral purpose,

---

[373] Magna Carta (1215), esp. clauses 39–40. These demonstrate the medieval conviction that authority must be limited to protect subjects—particularly against arbitrary power.

[374] **Pope Leo XIII**, *Rerum Novarum* (1891), §§13–14. Leo affirms the father's authority as natural, moral, and ordered toward the good of the family rather than domination.

[375] **Christine de Pizan**, *The Book of the Body Politic* (1407). De Pizan explicitly compares the queen to the heart of the political body, emphasizing her formative and stabilizing role.

[376] **St. Paul**, *Epistle to the Galatians* 3:28 (dignity before God), read alongside Ephesians 5–6, which maintains distinction of roles without denying dignity.

the family weakens, and societies that undermine it inevitably decay alongside it.[377] Where the family is dissolved, freedom does not expand; it collapses into isolation, dependency, and disorder.

---

[377] **Pope Pius XI**, *Divini Illius Magistri* (1929), §§7–9; *They Have Uncrowned Him*, **Archbishop Marcel Lefebvre**, ch. 1–2. Both argue that modern liberalism undermines society by dissolving the family's authority and moral function.

Part 5: Restoring the Wisdom of Christendom

Chapter 13: What the Modern World Can Learn from Catholic Monarchy

Above all else, the modern world suffers primarily from a loss of meaning. Politics has been stripped of its sacred character and reduced to a mechanism for distributing power, managing resources, and arbitrating competing desires. In the process, authority has ceased to be moral and has become merely procedural. Laws are enforced, but no longer revered. Offices are filled, but no longer honored. Power persists, but it no longer understands why it exists.

Christian monarchy rested on a radically different understanding. Political authority was not self-justifying, nor was it derived from popular will. It was understood as a participation in divine order, bound by moral law and oriented toward the formation of souls. Kings ruled not because they were strongest or most popular, but because they stood beneath God and were publicly accountable to

Him. Their legitimacy did not come from consent alone, but from consecration. To govern was not merely to command, but to answer.

This sacral understanding of politics imposed real limits on power. A king could not redefine good and evil, nor could he legislate against nature without consequence. Divine law stood above royal law, just as royal law stood above custom. The king's rule was personal, moral, and stable in a way modern regimes cannot easily replicate.

At the heart of this system was a paternal conception of authority. The king was not an abstract administrator, but the political father of his people. Like a father within the household, his authority existed not to dominate, but to provide, protect, correct, and preserve. He was expected to think in generations rather than election cycles, to guard inheritance rather than exploit resources, and to restrain his own appetites for the sake of those entrusted to him. Where authority today is increasingly anonymous and temporary, medieval kingship was visible, enduring, and morally exposed.

The modern rejection of paternal authority has not eliminated power; it has only rendered it unstable and impersonal. In abandoning the idea that rule must answer to divine law and resemble fatherhood, modern politics has severed authority from responsibility. The result is not freedom, but rule without accountability, law without meaning, and power without love. To understand what Christian monarchy can teach us, we must first recover this lost truth: political order cannot be neutral. It must either be sacred, or it will become predatory.

Chapter 14: The Future of Political Order

In recent years, I have come to identify politically as a neo-medievalist, if not a Chestertonian. That said, I write this book not to romanticize the past, but to awaken readers to the wisdom and beauty of medieval European society. It would be impossible to recreate the past, and I would not advocate for such an attempt. Instead, I hope to persuade as many minds as possible to take part in forming a new society, a new Christendom: one inspired by the past, informed by the present, and fortified against the future. The central question posed by neo-medievalism is not *"How do we go back?"* but rather, *"What truths did we abandon, and how might they be restored?"* Catholic monarchy, understood in this light, is not a museum piece, but a case study in ordered authority, one capable of illuminating a blueprint for a more humane, stable, and joyful society. The failure of modern systems stems from far more than flawed policies; their dysfunction reveals a collapse of moral architecture.

Amid the ruin, it is the duty of Christians not merely to critique, but to rebuild.

What follows, then, is not a call for nostalgia, but for recovery. The restoration of subsidiarity, local authority, and intermediate institutions is not a regression, but a return to political sanity. Medieval society functioned because it understood that freedom cannot survive when all authority is centralized, abstract, and distant. Authentic liberty flourishes only when power is rooted close to the people: in families, parishes, guilds, towns, and regions. Where obligation is personal and authority intelligible. Modern states promise freedom through uniformity and central administration; Christendom achieved it through variety, custom, and layered responsibility.

Likewise, political renewal cannot occur apart from tradition, law, and religion. Law divorced from moral truth becomes coercion, while tradition severed from faith hardens into empty habit. Medieval political life endured because it acknowledged that authority is not self-created, but received, mediated through nature, and embodied in concrete institutions. To reject this is not to become neutral, but to enthrone a different metaphysics, one in which power answers only to itself.

I have come to understand that feudal monarchy, at least as it developed in the Christian West, was far and away superior to every modern alternative. I do not claim sufficient knowledge to judge every civilization by the same standard. Yet I suspect that most cultures flourish best when governed according to analogous principles rather than identical forms. Japan's imperial system, for example, long preserved hierarchy, ritual, continuity, and reverence without erasing its unique cultural identity. Catholic political thought has never demanded uniformity of culture, only conformity to truth.

Indeed, the traditional Catholic vision is not to flatten the world into a single civilization, but to bring all nations into harmony with Christ and His Church, each according to its own character. Catholicism is universal not because it destroys difference, but because it fulfills it. As several Catholic thinkers have observed in various forms, God desires many nations united by one true religion, while the devil seeks many religions under a single, centralized power. Philosophically, the reason is clear: truth unifies without erasing distinction, while error fragments belief even as it concentrates control. Where divine law reigns, diversity can flourish in order. Where truth is denied, power must compensate through force and uniformity.

This is why modern regimes, despite their rhetoric of tolerance, tend toward cultural homogenization, bureaucratic centralization, and ideological enforcement. Without a shared moral order above the state, unity must be manufactured. Christendom required no such fabrication. It rested on a common faith that allowed political authority to remain limited, local, and humane.

What this book ultimately proposes is not a single blueprint imposed upon all peoples, but a flexible, organic recovery of principles: one attentive to place, history, and human scale. As Chesterton argued in *The Outline of Sanity*, a healthy society does not demand that all men live the same way, but that all men have the genuine freedom to live well according to their nature and gifts. A future order worthy of man will not be mass-produced. It will be built town by town, charter by charter, family by family, until authority once again serves life, rather than consuming it

The restoration of monarchy, if it ever occurs, will not be the result of a sudden political revolution or the declaration of a constitution. Historically, kingship did not arise because men decided they wanted a king; it arose because society had already formed the moral, cultural, and religious conditions that made kingship intelligible, legitimate, and necessary. The anointing of a royal line by the Church was never the beginning of monarchy, but its confirmation. Before a crown could be placed on a head, a people had to exist who understood authority as something sacred and ordered toward the common good.

In Christendom, royal anointing signified three realities at once. First, that authority comes from God, not from numbers, force, or ideology. Second, that the king was bound by divine and moral law, not above it. Third, that the ruler existed for the people, not the people for the ruler. The Church did not create kings from nothing; she recognized families and leaders who had already demonstrated continuity, service, protection, and legitimacy over time. A royal house emerged organically long before it was crowned.

For such a reality to re-emerge, profound cultural shifts would be required. Society would need to recover a belief in objective truth, natural hierarchy, and moral obligation. Authority would need to be seen once again as a burden rather than a privilege. The modern obsession with equality of function would have to give way to an acceptance of differentiated roles rooted in nature, competence, and responsibility. Above all, political life would need to be re-sacralized: not in the sense of clerical domination, but in the recognition that law and power answer to something higher than themselves.

Yet none of this means that we are powerless in the present. As Chesterton observed, refusing the big shop and choosing the small one may appear insignificant, but it is still resistance, and resistance multiplied becomes culture. One Catholic living distributively is a gesture. Millions living that way would constitute an alternative civilization.

The deeper problem of Catholic influence is not merely political structure, but spiritual apathy. Many Catholics today live scarcely differently from their secular neighbors. Liberal assumptions are absorbed uncritically. The faith is reduced to sentiment, ritual without formation, or ethics without metaphysics. This is precisely what Archbishop Lefebvre and Bishop Richard Williamson criticized: a watered-down Catholicism incapable of shaping culture because it no longer demands coherence, sacrifice, or courage. A people that does not know what it believes cannot govern itself, let alone sustain a civilization.

If Catholics were to take their faith seriously again, not merely privately, but socially, certain changes would follow almost inevitably. Families would reassert authority over education. Parishes would regain centrality in daily life. Guild-like economic associations would emerge naturally wherever people shared work, craft, and obligation. These would all follow from Catholics once again living as though their faith was true, not merely hypothetical.

As modern systems continue to strain under their own contradictions, and they will, because they depend on debt, abstraction, and the fragility of centralization, life will become harder, not easier. The cost of food, housing, and energy already points in this direction. When global supply chains falter, bureaucracies fail, and currencies weaken, the ability to produce locally will cease to be a lifestyle choice and become a requirement for survival. Historically, this is always how order returns: not through ideology, but through necessity.

Here lies one of the greatest injustices of the modern world: that even peasants and serfs once possessed access to land, while many modern families do not. If Catholics are to rebuild anything resembling a humane order, land access will be essential. This need not mean violent expropriation or state redistribution. It could begin modestly: shared land trusts, cooperative farms, parish-supported agriculture, monastic partnerships, and intentional rural communities. Catholics providing land access to one another would not merely be solving an economic problem, but restoring a moral one: rooting families in place, responsibility, and inheritance.

Over time, such arrangements could resemble a postmodern Catholic feudalism: not identical to the medieval past, but animated by the same principles: personal authority, reciprocal obligation, land-based security, and moral restraint. Lords would not be corporate boards or technocrats, but families or institutions known by name. Authority would be visible, answerable, and embedded in community.

This stands in stark contrast to the technocratic feudalism already emerging: a world of digital serfdom, surveillance, algorithmic control, and transhumanist aspirations, where ownership is replaced by subscription, labor by dependency, and identity by data. In that system, hierarchy exists without responsibility, power without face, and control without love. It is feudalism without fatherhood.

The restoration of monarchy, if it ever comes, would likely occur only after such organic orders had already taken root. A royal line would not be proclaimed; it would be recognized. The Church would anoint not a charismatic figure, but a family that had already proven stewardship over land and people across generations. This would not happen everywhere, nor all at once. It might begin in one region, one nation, perhaps even one city-state. And it would happen only if God wills it.

History is not controlled by systems, but by Providence. Our task is not to force outcomes, but to live rightly within our limits: to rebuild where we stand, to resist where we can, and to hand on something better than we received. If monarchy returns, it will not be because men demanded it, but because they had once again become worthy of it.

www.ingramcontent.com/pod-product-compliance
Lightning Source LLC
LaVergne TN
LVHW090415210926
848480LV00002B/578